STUCK IN THE TRENCHES
WELCOME TO THE DISTRICT OF COLOMBIA

HUFF THA GREAT

URBAN AINT DEAD

URBAN AINT DEAD
P.O Box 960780
Riverdale GA., 30296

Cover Design: Angel Bearfield / Dynasty Cover Me

Edited By: Veronica Rena Miller / Red Diamond Editing by V. Rena, LLC / reddiamondediting5@yahoo.com

URBAN AINT DEAD and coinciding logo(s) are registered properties.

Contact Author on IG: @ifl_huff

Contact Publisher at www.urbanaintdead.com

Email: urbanaintdead@gmail.com

Print ISBN: 979-8-9875422-7-9

Ebook ISBN: 979-8-9875422-8-6

SOUNDTRACK

Scan the QR Code below to listen to the Soundtracks/Singles of some of your favorite U.A.D titles:

Don't have Spotify or Apple Music?
No Sweat!
Visit your choice streaming platform and search URBAN AINT DEAD.
Currently on lock serving a bid?
JPay, iHeartRadio, WHATEVER!
We got you covered.
Simply log into your facility's kiosk or tablet, go to music and search
URBAN AINT DEAD.

URBAN AINT DEAD

Like & Follow us on social media:
FB – URBAN AINT DEAD
IG: @urbanaintdead
Tik Tok - @urbanaintdead

SUBMISSION GUIDELINES

Submission Guidelines
Submit the first three chapters of your completed manuscript to
urbanaintdead@gmail.com, subject line: Your book's title. The
manuscript must be in a .doc file and sent as an attachment. The
document should be in Times New Roman, double-spaced and in size
12 font. Also, provide your synopsis and full contact information. If
sending multiple submissions, they must each be in a separate email.
Have a story but no way to submit it electronically? You can still
submit to URBAN AINT DEAD. Send in the first three chapters,
written or typed, of your completed manuscript to:
URBAN AINT DEAD

P.O Box 960780
Riverdale GA., 30296

DO NOT send original manuscript. Must be a duplicate.
Provide your synopsis and a cover letter containing your full contact
information.

Thanks for considering URBAN AINT DEAD.

ACKNOWLEDGMENTS

Let me start off by sayin' I'm blessed to be in this position.

I.F.L, I'm still standing on the business. I'd like to thank everyone reading this book for supporting me. Thank you.

To all my haters, fuck you, and a big fuck you to the author Ghost. Fuck you, you wild creep ass nigga.

Now, let's get back to business…

I'd like thank URBAN AINT DEAD for giving me a platform and believing in a nigga. The book game is ours. Believe that! To all the men and women behind the wall, in the struggle, doing this mother-fucker, I see you. Our day coming, too.

Raven, I love you, Baby. Eight years down, we still thuggin', grindin', building our platform. I love you forever. You know that. To young Huff Tha Great, you going to the N.F.L. Daddy so proud of you, Big Dog. But until you make it I'ma buy you any and everything you want. You know daddy rich. I love you, Big Huff. Shout-out to Po. Welcome home! It's your time, Slim! I'll be there soon.

So without further ado, let me get to this street shit—Oh, before I forget, me and a couple niggas in here read a book from the author Chris Green called *Midnight Cartel* that shit was trash. Step your pen game up.

Anthony Fields, what's up, Slim!?

D.C stand up!

Trinidad stand up!

U.A.D, it's the motherfuckin' takeover! We here now!

Let's get back to the trenches…

D.C. GLOSSARY

1. Dogs – guns
2. Multified – high as shit
3. Moe, Slim, or Bob – Slang name for someone
4. Braced – to rob a person
5. Flushing, Crushing – to kill someone
6. Lunching – Tripping

PROLOGUE

"GOT DAMN MOE, how long does it take to count money?" Savage asked, pacing back and forth in the abandoned house. He walked from the window to the door and looked out.

"Chill soldier, let me do this... everything good, baby," Deon replied, looking up from the table with an irritated look on his face.

Savage looked at Deon, watching him as he sat the last stack on the table. Savage turned back to the window and looked out the blinds to make sure the law or a move wasn't lurking. See what Deon didn't know was every time Savage turned his head, Savage peeped him sliding money in his pocket on the low.

"Wild ass nigga gon' make me flush his ass," Savage said to himself, debating on whipping out right then and crushing Deon and taking everything. Savage was about to say fuck it until he heard his name.

"Aye, Young Savage, let's wrap this shit up," Deon said as he stood up and put his 44 on his hip. He put the last stack in a black book bag, glanced at Savage, and thought, *"I ain't paying you shit. Soon as we pull up to your car, I'm crushing your young ass."* Deon laughed to himself as he picked up the book bag and walked towards the door.

"How much is it?" Savage asked as he followed Deon to the door.

"Just chill baby, I got you. You gon' get your cut." Deon replied with irritation in his voice as he opened the front door. The winter air hit them as soon as they stepped into the street. It was almost pitch black due to the people in the neighborhood shooting out the street-lights so the law couldn't see them at night. "Damn, it's cold," Deon said as he walked quickly to his car. It was cold, but Savage didn't feel it. His adrenaline was rushing as he took the Glock 17 off his hip and walked towards Deon. "Damn... it's freezing." Deon blew into his hands as he rubbed them together before he stuck the key in his car door.

Savage raised up the 17, "Aye, Deon!" Savage yelled.

"What?" Deon yelled as he looked towards Savage and saw a flash.

Blocka!

The first shot hit Deon in the face, making him fall as his blood flew all over his car door. Savage ran up and stood over him.

Blocka! Blocka! Blocka!

The shots echoed loudly as bullets hit Deon in his head and face. Savage grabbed the book bag and snatched the 44 off Deon's hip and ran off into the night thinking, "Fuck that bitch ass nigga!"

An older man was in the kitchen when the first shots went off. He walked to the window and witnessed the murder. He just shook his head, turned off the kitchen lights, and went to bed. Murder wasn't anything new; it was the norm. Everybody knew to mind their business and never talk to the police. That was the law of the land; let the streets deal with the streets.

ONE
SAVAGE

"THIS IS D.C. NEWS, *reporting live from Wellington Park where the body of Deon Smith, age 27, was found gunned down early this morning. Deon Smith died from multiple gunshot wounds to the head and neck area. This marks the five hundredth murder this year. The police have no leads at this time. If anyone has any information that can lead to an arrest, please contact the police at 1-800-Crimestoppers."*

"Fuck that bitch ass nigga!" Savage yelled out loud as he blew a thick cloud of smoke in the air. "Cool 15 free bands," Savage said, laughing as he grabbed the PS5 controller. He went to YouTube and cut on Moneybagg Yo's videos. *"I'm trending, my belt, my shoes, my shirt this shit come from Fendi..."* Savage rapped as he hit the J a couple of times, blowing smoke out of his nose as he watched his Aunt J walk into his room.

"Savage, what the fuck I tell you about smoking and not lighting a got damn incense? And Aunt J need some money," she said, leaning on the door, looking from the stack of money on the table to Savage, with a smirk on her face.

Aunt J was an all-around junkie. Crack, heroin, and tricking was what she was known for. The streets had nicknamed her Superhead. Aunt J was a gangsta even though she had her vices. She'd been in the streets so long; she had seen and been through everything. Aunt J was 43 years old, with a cute Jada Pinkett face and a nice body to go with it. You could tell she was bad back in her day. She took Savage in when he didn't have anywhere to go or turn to.

Young Savage was what you call a product of his environment. He was born and raised in the street. His mother was a dope fiend, and she was one of the best boosters in the city. His father's name was Big Savage. He was a dope fiend, one of those getting money, gangsta ass dope fiends. He was a taker, a robber, that was his M.O. Everybody in the city knew what was up with Big Savage. If you had it, he was coming... flat out. From the age of seven, they had Young Savage stealing stashes, by 10 he witnessed his first murder. At the age of 13, Big Savage had put a .22 in his hands. "Fuck school, get it how you live," were his words of wisdom.

Savage's life changed when he was 14 years old. On July 7, 2014, he was with Big Savage and would never forget that day. Big Savage and Young Savage were on their way to the barbershop. They pulled up on West Virginia Ave. and parked in front of Cuts Barbershop. Big Savage was gone off some good heroin. He always told Savage to keep his eyes on the mirrors and his surroundings at all times, no matter what. He couldn't let any of those suckas catch him lacking. This day, when Big Savage parked, the heroin he got from up the Gardens was a missile. It had Big Savage's head in his lap.

Young Savage took his eyes off the mirrors and his surroundings to shake Big Savage out of his nod. He'd been so preoccupied with aiding his dad, he missed the person sliding up on the car until he heard the shot. He heard the glass breaking and felt blood fly all over his face. Young Savage was stuck in shock as he and the killer locked eyes. The killer upped, pointing the pistol at Young Savage.

Young Savage closed his eyes and when he opened them, the killer was gone. Big Savage was slumped over, his head lay on the steering wheel, bleeding out. His brains were on the dashboard, and blood was everywhere. The only thing he had to remember his father by was his "Savage Shit" chain. It was all gold with VVS diamonds dancing through it. After that day, Savage never went anywhere without it.

Six months later, Savage came home and found his mother in the bathroom with a needle sticking out of her arm... dead from an over-dose. Aunt J took Savage in, they needed each other. She was in the streets, down bad, tricking hard, sucking and fucking anybody for a hit before Savage came into the picture. Now, she didn't have to trick anymore because Savage made sure she was straight.

He knew what was up and never judged her. He needed her too. After his parents died, his heart turned cold. He didn't love or care about anything but money and his guns. Aunt J gave him someone to care about, slowing him down a little bit. She gave him law and taught him the ins and outs of the street game.

"Here Aunt J," Savage grabbed the stack of money off the table, counted off a band, and handed it to her.

"Thank you, baby!" Aunt J saluted, smiling as she put the money in her robe's pocket. "Look at you, looking just like your got damn daddy." She said, laughing. "Be careful out here Savage, always follow your instincts. Shoot first, ask questions later. Even if you're wrong, let God judge that when you get there. It's about living another day on this earth, Love you, Young Savage. I'm about to get my wake-up blast." She reminded him and blew him a kiss as she walked out of his room.

1:00 P.M

"Point made, Point made, we ain't with the subliminals, if you play, we going finish you." Savage rapped to Moneybagg Yo as he got his shower clothes together. He went to grab his towel, nodding his head to the music when Freaky busted through the door.

"Fuck is up?" Freaky yelled.

Savage jumped and reached in his shorts pocket for his X-D. His heart was drumming in his chest, thinking it was a move.

"Fuck is up with you, Moe?" Savage yelled out, mad as he let his X-D go and looked at Freaky with that "you lunching" look.

"Shut your 'noid ass up," Freaky laughed as he laid on Savage's bed.

Freaky was five years older than Savage. He was 23, 6'2, and a 200-pound Trey Songz looking motherfucker. Freaky rocked all those hitting ass fades and was dripping. Everything was foreign. His aura said "workhorse." All he did was hit licks, take dogs, get money, fuck bitches, and backdoor shit. He got the name Freaky because he was a freaky nigga for real.

He didn't deal with anybody but Savage and that's because they had history. All robberies and work call shit. He started hanging with Savage right after Big Savage got killed. Savage was running the streets crazy, robbing everything in the city. Freaky ain't fuck with nobody else, everybody was free picks. If you were up, and he caught you lacking, you were going in the trunk. Freaky was from Congress Park but was known all over the city.

"Your shit lucky," Savage looked at Freaky, still mad as he grabbed his towel. "I was bout to flush your ass."

"Fuck all that shit." Freaky waved Savage off and pulled out an ounce of cookie and some sheets. He took out some buds, put them in the sheet, and looked at Savage while he was twisting up. "Fuck happened with that Deon shit? I saw the face on the news." He asked while firing up a J.

"Oh yeah," Savage said excitedly. "The move went smooth. Kill, I caught the nigga De-De soon as he was coming out of the trap, crept up on him, upped the dog... the nigga almost shitted on himself looking down the barrel of that big ass Glock 17." Savage laughed as he sat down on the bed. "Me and your wild ass man, Deon, get up to Wellington Park to count the paper, Deon taking all day and shit. So, I'm like 'fuck it, let me see if this nigga playing these stupid ass games.' I fake walk to the bathroom, I peeked and saw the nigga sliding money in his pocket."

"What?" Freaky yelled and busted out laughing with smoke coming out of his nose as he passed the J to Savage.

"Shit ain't funny. I was bout to flush the nigga right there but I ain't want all that blood on the money and shit. My mind was already made up I was crushing his ass, flat out." Savage inhaled a big cloud of smoke and blew it in the air. "This shit gas," he passed the J back to Freaky. "So, look!" Savage yelled, getting up and pacing the room, high as shit. "I'm pacing, looking out the window, the wild ass nigga still sliding money in his pocket on the low and in my face!" he yelled while shaking his head as he paced, reliving that day.

Freaky was high off the cookie, smiling and looking at Savage thinking, *''Shorty shit too turned.''*

"But that ain't even what did it," Savage looked at Freaky with a serious expression. "I asked the nigga what's the count, he talking bout, 'you gon' get your cut'... like I'm sweet. I let the stupid nigga walk in front of me. Soon as he got to his car, I crushed his ass, took all the money and the dog off him. I came up on 15 bands, a free 44, and one less wild nigga in the city," Savage boasted while leaning on the wall looking at Freaky.

Freaky finished the J and put it in the ashtray. He looked at Savage with his eyes red and low. Freaky was high as shit.

"Fuck that nigga." Freaky lifted up his Dior hoodie.

"Look what I came up on," Freaky said taking a dog off his hip. "This the Glock 18 with the 36 in it." He handed it to Savage.

Savage was geeking, when he saw the leg in it. It had the fully and the auto switch on the side of it.

"Let me get this, Moe." Savage asked with his hand still gripping the 18.

"That's you, Slim. What's up? You still want me to drop you off? Your lil ass need to hurry up. I got shit to do." Freaky stood up, walked to the PlayStation and put Grand Theft Auto 5 in the PS5.

"Alright, let me fuck with this shower real quick." Savage grabbed his clothes and walked to the bathroom, taking the 18 with him.

2:50 P.M

Savage hopped out of the shower and got dressed, threw on some skinny light blue Balmain jeans, a light blue Dior hoodie, and some butters. He put his flats in his ears, Savage Shit chain around his neck, and $7500 in each of his pockets. He put the 18 on his hip, his Dior trench on, and looked at Freaky, who was firing up another sheet of gas as they walked out of the apartment. As soon as they stepped in the hallway they ran into Lil Mya and Dawn.

Mya was dark-skinned, cool in the face, but her body was flat out. She was thick, with big titties, big thighs, and a phat ass. She was a stallion.

Dawn was cute in the face, 5'4, petite body with a plump ass, and nice palmable titties. Dawn looked good, however, she was just ghetto, burned out off the gas, and had a couple of bodies under her belt.

"Damn Mya," Freaky flirted, looking at her standing in the hallway door in some all-black leggings, looking phat as shit. You could see her thong print from the back.

"Boy," Mya said, blushing and looking Freaky up and down, loving what she saw, pussy getting moist. Freaky was Dior down, with a fresh fade, wrist, neck, and ears flooded. You could see the knots busting out of his pockets. It looked like he had on thigh pads.

"Boy, what?" Freaky asked, walking up to Mya. He hit the J, passed it to Savage, and then wrapped his arms around Mya's waist, palming her ass and whispering in her ear.

Savage was leaning on the wall hitting the J. Dawn leaned on him, telling him straight up that she wanted him to fuck the shit out of her. Savage blew smoke in the air as he grabbed her soft plump ass, dick getting hard.

"Come on," he grabbed her hand when the hallway door opened.

"Fuck is up?" Greg bellowed, walking in and seeing Freaky whispering in his girl's ear.

Mya jumped back and looked stupid.

Freaky just looked at Greg and his two men, Dog and Smoke. His hand went straight to his hip. Savage's hand went to his hip as he dropped the J and watched to see how everything played out. Savage had his mind made up that if they did any purping, he was crushing all of them.

Freaky watched Greg grab Mya by her hair and drag her out of the building, thinking, *this nigga a clown.*

"Get the fuck off her hair!" Dawn yelled, shaking her head. Dog and Smoke were looking at Freaky, and Freaky was looking back at them, mugging.

"Come on, Moe." Freaky urged Savage while still mugging Dog and Smoke, praying they said something.

"I'm a fuck you later," Savage vowed to Dawn as he gripped her ass one last time before he mugged on Dog and Smoke as he and Freaky walked out of the building.

Dog and Smoke were still looking but they didn't say anything.

"I should spank them bitch ass niggas right now," Freaky vented. His body told him to flush both of them as they walked to the 650. He saw Greg and Mya arguing up the block.

"Fuck them niggas. It ain't our fault we drippin' and their bitches trying to fuck." Savage said as they hopped in the 650.

Both of them put their guns on their laps, then Freaky started the car. Savage was watching the mirrors and his surroundings. Freaky looked towards the building and saw Smoke at the door mugging.

I'm crushing his ass, Freaky said to himself as he pulled off.

SMOKE AND DOG

"Bitch ass nigga!" Dog mouthed as he watched Freaky pull off.

"Y'all anything ass bitches on them niggas' dick!" Smoke shouted while looking at Dawn.

"Boy, fuck your dirty ass. You dirty as fuck!" she screamed, rolling her eyes as she walked to the door.

"Fuck you bitch!" Smoke kicked her in the ass as she walked out of the door.

"Bitch, I hope both y'all bitch ass niggas get kilt!" She yelled while holding her ass, mad as shit as she walked up the street.

"Next time I catch that nigga Freaky, I'ma down his ass. And Savage want to act like he with his man, he can get crushed, too. I'ma make Aunt J suck my dick, watch," Dog vented as they sat in the building waiting on a sell.

TWO
3:52 P.M

"I GOT a big boy lick lined up for us, Slim. I'm just putting the pieces together." Freaky told Savage as he pulled up in front of Mike's car lot. Freaky put the car in park, put his hand on his dog, and looked over at Savage. "Moe, I hate to be all in your business and shit but fuck, you need to leave that snake ass bitch Cat alone."

"Here you go," Savage said with his eyes on the mirrors, watching everything around him.

After Big Savage got killed, he made a promise to himself to never get caught lacking.

"Alright hardheaded ass nigga, listen..." Freaky looked Savage in his eyes. "If something happens to you, and you around that bitch Cat, I'm smoking her. Flat out!"

"Alright, Moe." Savage stated as he put the 18 on his hip, dapped Freaky up, and hopped out of the 650, not really trying to hear what Freaky was talking about.

Freaky just shook his head as he watched Savage walk in the car lot.

"Tender dick ass nigga," Freaky mumbled to himself as he pulled off.

———

Savage walked in the car lot and saw all types of cars. Lexus, Benzes, Audis, and Chargers were all on display. As he walked up to a smoke-grey Dodge Charger he heard his name called.

"Young Savage!"

Savage turned around and saw a smiling Big Mike walking out of his office. Big Mike was one of those old-head gangsters that ducked the grave and a jail cell. He saw a lot of good men lost in the streets when they became greedy. Big Mike took his cash and went legit. He was a "Sho nuff" nigga, and could get his hands on anything: work, guns, cars, you name it. Big Mike had a good name. He was a stand-up man in the city.

"Young Savage," Big Mike called again, smiling ear to ear because he knew that Savage was about to spend a little paper. Big Mike had known Savage since he was a child. He loved him but hated his father. He felt like Big Savage was cruddy and was glad when he got killed.

"What's up, Fat Boy?" Savage greeted him and dapped him up. "I want this joint." Savage pointed to the smoke grey Charger.

"You want that, you know that's the 2015 SRT?" Mike asked, putting his arms around Savage's shoulder. "Come to the office and get your paperwork, 90-day tags and keys."

Big Mike and Savage walked inside the dealership and made their way to his office. Pointing to a chair at his desk Big Mike said, "have a seat," and made his way to the back.

Savage liked Big Mike, but he wasn't doing no lacking. He sat down and put the 18 on his lap, finger on the trigger.

Fuck that, I ain't doing no lacking, he murmured to himself and relaxed as Big Mike came out of the back with the paperwork and a box in his hand.

Mike sat everything on the table. "Look, give me 10 for the car and three for this." Big Mike grabbed an F&N out of the box and handed it to Savage.

Savage grabbed the gun and examined it. He sat it down on the table and went into his pockets and counted out 13 bands. Big Mike smiled and thought about the 5 bands he'd just made off the deal.

FREAKY

BENNING PARK - 6:40 P.M.

"Bet back nigga," Nook said as he picked up his money out of the pot when his phone rang. Nook grabbed his phone and looked at the caller I.D. "Hold up, this a sell, I'll be right back." Nook jogged out of the building and answered his phone. "It's two niggas in the building. The guns are in the mailbox. Hurry up!" Nook told Freaky before he hung up and walked up the block.

Freaky parked the car and left it running. He checked the 5th, threw on his hood, grabbed a bag, and jumped out of the car. He walked up to the building, 5th in hand as he rushed in.

"Don't move!" Freaky yelled, waving the 5th at the crowd. "Lay face fucking down!"

"Alright, Slim," one guy said as he got down.

Freaky started picking money up off the floor when one of the guys tried to run to the mailbox. Freaky upped and hit him.

Blocka!

The bullet hit the guy in his stomach. Freaky ran and grabbed the two dogs out of the mailbox. He stuffed all of the money in his bag and ran out of the building, making eye contact with Nook. Nook waited until Freaky was in his car, whipped out and shot in the air to make it look good.

Nook ran in the building and saw his man holding his stomach, leaking... "Fuckkk!" Nook yelled, playing the role as he grabbed his phone and called for help. Freaky was already gone. Another day on the job.

THREE
SAVAGE - 8:40 P.M

"YEAH, *I'm young but got something to lose, in the streets I done paid all my dues.*" Lil Baby blasted out of the Charger's speakers as Savage pulled up in Woodland, parked, and hopped out with the 18 on his hip. He had the F&N sticking out of his trench coat's pocket, drinking Rosé out of the bottle. He nodded to a few people.

"Ay, boy," he heard girls calling, necking, trying to see who he was as he walked in Cat's building. As soon as he stepped in the building, he smelled gas in the air and saw three young niggas shooting dice on the hallway floor. The young niggas started reaching and his hand went straight to his F&N. He could see it in their eyes that to them, he was a move. An unfamiliar face on this side of town was fair game.

"Savage!" his man Floyd called, walking down the steps, Mac in his hand, coming to see what was going on.

"Floyd, what's up Moe?" Savage greeted him, nodded, and took a sip of Rosé. His hand was still on his F&N as he watched the young niggas, ready to squeeze if any of them moved wrong.

"Stand down. Slim, cool," Floyd demanded to Tim, Tom, and Go-Go. They took their hands off their guns, but they were still watching Savage.

"I'ma catch you later, Slim," Savage said to Floyd, still watching the young niggas as he walked up the steps.

"Who the fuck is that nigga? He look like a lick and that Savage shit chain hittin'. He lucky he yo man."

Savage was listening. His finger went around the trigger, his mind, heart, and body were telling him to walk down the steps and flat line all of them; but he took a deep breath and released it, thinking to himself how careless niggas could be at times. They had no idea the caliber of street nigga they were dealing with. They were dead, and didn't even know it.

Deciding to spare them, he laughed and took another sip from the bottle as he unlocked the door and stepped in, closing and locking the door behind him.

"Aye, Cat!" he called as he walked to her room. "Fuck this dumb ass bitch at? Bitch knew I was on my way," Savage said out loud, sitting the bottle of Rosé on the dresser. He took the F&N out of his trench coat and sat it beside the bottle. Savage took off his trench and walked to the closet, hanging it up. Then he grabbed a duffle bag and shoebox out of the closet and muttered to himself, "If a gun or dime missing, I'ma smoke this bitch!" He took the bags to the bed, sat the 18 on the bed, and turned on Young Dolph on his iPhone. He took all the money out and counted each dollar.

"Shit all here," he said, putting 25 bands back in the shoebox. He had 7 guns: a P90 Ruger, two Glocks, one 17, a 22, a Tec 22 with a 42 clip in it, a Drako with 100 round drum on it, and two Mac 11's. He added the 18 to the collection and put everything back in the closet. Savage locked the room's door, cut up the Dolph, and laid back on the bed sipping Rosé, twisting up some cookie.

FREAKY

CHOPPER CITY - 11:01 P.M.

Freaky was sitting in his 650, parked two buildings down from Savage's building. He had his .357 laying on his lap, with the seat laid back, watching Greg and Smoke sitting on the porch catching sells. Freaky had been parked in the same spot watching for the last hour. He was growing impatient and was thinking about just throwing on his mask, walking up to the porch, taping, and flushing both of them. He was about to do it but said, "Fuck it, I'll wait them out. The time's going to come."

———

"What you bout to do, Slim" Greg asked Smoke as he peeped up and down the block looking for sells. Greg looked at his watch and saw it was 11:10 p.m., he wanted to get up to Mya's house and get some pussy.

"Shit, I'm bout to slide up to Kim's joint. Shit slow, anyway." Smoke stood up and stretched. "I'ma comeback in the a.m., catch that early morning rush."

"No question." Greg stood, gave Smoke some dap, and started walking up the block.

Pulling out his phone, Smoke walked down the block towards Freaky's car.

———

Freaky watched as Smoke and Greg gave each other dap, and his heart rate sped up as he gripped his 357. He slid out the car, ducked down, and hid behind it.

Smoke was so focused on texting, he didn't peep Freaky until the .357 was in his face. Smoke's eyes got big, and he froze up, looking down the barrel of Freaky's 357.

"Fuck you!" Freaky pulled the trigger and the shot echoed, as a single bullet pierced Smoke's skull, sending him backwards head first. Freaky took off running before his body hit the pavement, brains leaking out on the sidewalk.

Hearing the shot, Greg thought about Smoke and called his phone but didn't get an answer. He tried again but got the same result.

I pray that wasn't Smoke, he thought as he turned and headed the way Smoked had walked.

In vain, of course…Smoke was already gone.

FOUR
WOODLAND - 12:10 A.M

BOOM! *Boom! Boom!*

"Open my fucking door, Savage." Savage jumped up out of his sleep, heart pounding in his chest. He grabbed the F&N off the table and looked around.

Boom! Boom!

"Alright, bitch hold up," Savage yelled, getting up off the bed and walking to the door with the F&N in his hand. He snatched the door open, and Cat was standing in the doorway smiling in just a pair of heels on her feet, looking sexy as shit.

Cat was 5'6, 160 pounds, and she rocked her hair in a short pixie cut. Her body was flawless. She had a nice phat, pretty ass with a gap between her legs, showing her phat, plump hairless pussy. Cat had big titties that sat up on her chest with big brown, pointy lickable nipples. They called her Cat because of her grey-green eyes. She was 36 years old and had been around for years. She'd witnessed the rise and fall of the best of them and only fucked with boss niggas that were up.

Cat stripped, boosted, committed fraud, and set up plays. Whatever was needed to get money. She never thought she would mess with a youngin' like Savage, but she saw his heart and knew she could use a stand-up young nigga like him. She caught Savage young, put that pussy and head on him, and had him hooked. Cat did her, but she really loved Savage and knew she could get him to do anything for her so that was a plus.

"Savage, who you talking to?" She asked, looking him in the eyes as she pushed him against the wall.

She dropped to her knees and pulled Savage's dick out of his pants. As soon as she put his dick in her mouth, Savage dropped the F&N on the floor and palmed her head. Savage knew Cat was a THOT, but she had him. She put him on 30 and 40 band licks, sucked and fucked him like a king, and turned up his swag. It was hard for him to leave her alone.

"Damn," Savage moaned, closing his eyes as Cat slid his dick all the way down her throat. She slid his dick to the tip of her lips, gazed into his eyes, and smiled as she sucked just the tip. Cat stood up, holding Savage's dick as she turned around facing the wall. She rubbed his dick up and down her pussy, then bent over and let Savage slide all the way in her pussy.

"Oh, Lil Boy, yesssss fuck me," Cat moaned as Savage held her waist and pounded her pussy. "Deeper baby, deeper Savage," Cat screamed, hands on the wall. Looking over her shoulder at Savage making sexy fuck-faces, she threw her ass back at him. Cat pushed back, letting Savage's dick go as far as it could go in her, and started grinding. Savage's whole mid-section was wet as pussy juice dripped down her thighs.

"I'm a cum on that dick, daddy, Oh my fucking ahhh!" Cat screamed as she came hard all over Savage's dick.

Savage pounded two more times, closed his eyes, and came deep in Cat's pussy. He slid to the floor holding Cat's waist, dick still in her as he sat on the floor trying to catch his breath. Cat was still grinding in a circle, creaming all over his dick.

"This pussy too good, Lil Boy," Cat boasted, smiling as she stood up when Savage's dick slid out of her pussy.

She walked off with nut cream rolling down her thighs. Savage was sitting in the same spot, drained, watching Cat walk up to him with a wet rag in her hand. She grabbed Savage's dick and wiped it clean. Putting his dick in his pants, he picked up the F&N, stood, walked in Cat's room, and laid on the bed. Cat looked at Savage laughing as she grabbed the J out of the ashtray. She fired it up, thinking, *I got a missile between my legs.* She climbed on the bed and sat on Savage's chest, pussy still warm. She hit the J and blew smoke in the air while looking in Savage's face.

"I was just up at Black's trap buying some weed… when I walked in, him and Cash were sitting at the table counting up big money, baby." Cat looked him in the eyes as she handed him the J.

"Kill, how much you think it was?" Savage hit the J and sat up, mind racing, getting excited.

"You know them niggas be trying to fuck. So, when I came in, Black got to showing off and shit. Talkin' bout that was a hunnid bands. I just glanced. You know I know money, Boo. I don't know if it was a hunnid, but it's *some* money. I saw big 50s and 100s," Cat detailed while finishing off the J and sitting the roach in the ashtray.

"You think they still up there?"

"Hell yeah, I just left there twenty minutes ago."

Right after I let Black's little dick ass fuck for a band, Cat mused to herself as she got up off of Savage.

Savage walked to the closet and grabbed his shoes, hoodie, ski mask, and 17 out of the duffle bag. Cat walked to the window, money on her mind, knowing it was at least 50 bands in that house. She knew they were about to come up.

That was another reason she fell in love with Savage. She knew his mind was stuck on go. He wasn't doing any bluffing and wasn't seeing anything or anybody. He was about that money. A *real* nigga. And Cat loved her a *real nigga.* That shit made her pussy wet.

"Look." Savage threw on his hoodie, put the 17 in his pocket, and rolled the ski mask on the top of his head while looking at Cat. "Who else was in there other than Black and Cash, and who was in the building?"

"Nobody. I watched Floyd, Tim, and Tom walking out of the building when I walked in. Listen, Boo." Cat looked at Savage. "I'm about to call your phone now as I watch the window. If I see some-thing that's looking wild, I'ma tell you."

"Bet." Savage nodded his head. "What's the building and apartment number?"

"1105, apartment 4," Cat squeaked out while grabbing her phone.

Savage put his hood on his head, right hand around the 17, and grabbed his phone. Putting it to his ear, he left out of the apartment. Savage was on high alert, watching his surroundings as he stepped out of the building.

It was quiet on the streets, a ghost town. Savage didn't even see a junkie as he made his way to building 1105. "Call Black now," Savage ordered Cat and hung up. He put the phone in his pocket as he stepped in Black's building. Savage was gripping the 17 with his finger on the trigger. He pulled his mask down just as he made it to apartment 4. Putting his back on the wall, he faced the steps just in case someone walked up.

"Aye, Cash, the bitch Cat on her way back up here." Being that there were only two inside, Savage knew it was obviously Black speaking.

He knocked.

"Matter fact, that's the bitch right there," Black said when he heard a knock on the door. He stood from the table. "You better get some of that pussy. Shit a torch." Black walked pass Cash, seated on the living room couch, grabbing big stacks of money off the coffee table and putting it in a book bag.

"I'ma let the bitch suck my dick," Cash replied, laughing as Black continued on to the door.

Savage heard the door unlock, and his adrenaline started rushing as he slid the 17 out of his hoodie. As soon as the door opened, Savage jammed the 17 in Black's face.

"Don't scream. Where that bag at?" Savage grabbed Black by his collar, pushed him in the house, and kicked the door closed behind him. You could see the shock and fear written all over Black's face as Savage pushed him in the living room. Cash looked up confused, then jumped up and started reaching. Savage pointed the 17 at him.

"If you move or pull out, I'm downin' you. Don't turn a robbery into a homicide. I just want the cash. Put your hands in the air now!" Savage yelled with his gun still pointed at Cash. He searched Black and didn't find anything. Cash and Black made eye contact and Black mouthed, *It's just money, Cash.* Cash nodded and put his hands up mad as shit on the inside.

Savage swung the 17 and hit Black in his head, causing him to fall down face first and hold his head.

"Lay on your stomach," Savage demanded.

Cash was mugging Savage, looking at his masked face as he got down on one knee. Black was still on the floor holding his head.

I'll make that shit back. I ain't dying over no money, he thought.

"On your stomach!" Savage yelled, getting impatient.

Cash looked at Savage and tried to reach for his dog, and Savage pulled the trigger.

Blocka!

The bullet hit Cash in his stomach, making him fall back on the couch, breathing hard, holding his bloody stomach.

"Bitch ass nigga!" Savage ran up to Cash, putting the 17 in his face. He pulled the trigger.

Boom!

The top side of Cash's head exploded, and blood sprayed the couch. Black was shaking, scared to death. He was too scared to look up. Savage grabbed the bag off the table and opened it.

"Jackpot!" It was full of money. Gripping the bag tightly, Savage ran out of the apartment.

Cat was sitting at the window when she heard the shots and peeked out just in time to see Savage run out of the building. She ran to the door and opened it.

Savage ran into Cat's building, up the stairs, and straight pass her into her apartment. She slammed the door behind him, and he didn't stop running until he was in Cat's room. She asked no questions; just shut the door, locked it, and ran straight to the kitchen.

Savage dropped the bag and started taking off all of his bloody clothes. Cat knew the routine. She came in the room with a trash bag and put Savage's clothes and Glock 17 in it. Wrapping it up, she ran out of the apartment.

Savage walked to the closet and put on a pair of shorts and a T-shirt. He grabbed the F&N, put on his shoes, and stood by the window watching the street.

As soon as Cat came back in the room, Savage told her to count the money and twist up.

"Alright, baby," Cat agreed as she dumped the money on the floor, glancing at Savage. *I love this young nigga,* she thought, her pussy moist as she began counting.

Savage was blowing gas watching the police pull up. He watched them tape off the building, question people, and take Cash's body out on a gurney with a white sheet over him.

Hours later, the streets were clear. Cat emerged from her room naked and approached him. Savage sat the F&N on the table and stood. She grabbed his hand and led him to the bathroom.

"How much was it?" Savage asked when they arrived.

"57 thousand, baby!" She screeched while taking off his clothes.

They got in the shower. Cat cleaned him up and sucked and fucked him until they passed out.

FLOYD - 1:41 A.M

Floyd was at the bottom of the building getting his dick sucked by a junkie when he heard the shots, pulled his dick out of the junkie's mouth, and was about to go investigate when he saw a masked man running in a building with a bag in his hand. Floyd didn't have a gun on him, so he stayed in the shadows and watched the man run in Cat's building.

Floyd watched Cat come out of the apartment twenty minutes later with a trash bag in her hands. As soon as he saw Cat run back in the building, he gave the junkie a stone and ran out of the building to see what the fuck was going on.

FIVE
FREAKY
CHOPPER CITY - 1:53 A.M.

AFTER FREAKY KILLED SMOKE, he ran straight to Savage's house. As soon as he walked in the house, he smelled crack in the air and saw Aunt J speed-walking out of the room in just a nightgown. Aunt J was coming to see who had entered her house.

"Freaky?" Aunt J called, coming down off her high, watching as Freaky shut and locked the door behind him.

"It's me," Freaky said as he walked up, grabbed Aunt J's arm, and pulled her to him.

Freaky slid his finger under her nightgown and saw that she didn't have on any panties. Freaky started finger-fucking her wet pussy from the back.

"Ooohh" Aunt J moaned, biting her bottom lip as the sensation started to feel good.

"Suck my dick for me, Aunt J," Freaky whispered in Aunt J's ear as he dropped his pants to his ankles.

Aunt J knew it was wrong. She told Freaky a year ago that she wasn't doing that no more, but the crack had her horny. She hadn't fucked or sucked a dick in 6 months, and just couldn't help herself.

She massaged Freaky's dick. "Don't tell Savage." Dropping to her knees, she put it in her mouth. Freaky leaned back on the wall, palmed her head, and let her work.

WOODLAND

FLOYD AND BLACK - 11:02 A.M

As soon as Floyd found out that Cash got killed and robbed, he put two-and-two together and called Black's phone ASAP. Black was stressed, messed up about his right-hand man getting killed. He wanted answers. Black met up with Floyd in the McDonald's parking lot on Naylor Road.

As soon as Floyd hopped in the truck, he dapped Black up and told him, "I was in Cat's building last night and saw a nigga with a mask on running up to her apartment with a bag in his hands." Black looked over at Floyd, listening. "I really ain't think shit about it. I knew the nigga Savage be hittin' licks and be fuckin' with Cat, but I ain't think he'd pull no shit like that. I watched Cat come out her apartment with a trash bag in her hand. I put 2 and 2 together. The nigga Savage did that shit, and Cat pulled the play!"

"That snake ass bitch," Black roared, remembering Cat calling him right before it happened. "Stupid ass bitch pulled the play. I got they ass, watch. I got'em."

Black started up the car and pulled off with murder in his heart.

SAVAGE

WOODLAND - 11:40 A.M.

"This is D.C. News, last night marks the 520th murder of the year. Last night, at 2:00 am, Rashad Cash, age 32, was shot and killed in what police call a drug deal gone wrong. Police have no leads at this time. It's a $1,000 reward for any information that leads to an arrest. If you have any information, please contact the police at 1-800-Crimestoppers."

"No leads at this time," Savage declared, smiling as he got out the bed, grabbed his Savage Shit chain, and put it around his neck.

"Boy, you so damn press." Cat smiled as she looked at him while she laid on her stomach.

Cat grabbed Savage by his thigh and pulled him to her. She put his dick in her mouth and sucked it with no hands, pulling him deeper down her throat.

Loud, wet, slurps was all to be heard as Cat gave him that sloppy head. Savage leaned over and grabbed Cat's ass as he fucked her mouth. Cat's mouth was super wet, feeling like a pussy.

"Shit, Cat," Savage moaned as he palmed her head, closing his eyes and cumming down her throat. Savage's legs got weak, and he tried to pull his dick out of her mouth, but she smacked his hands and pulled him deeper into her mouth as she sucked him dry. "Fuckkk!" Savage groaned, snatching his dick out of her mouth, backing up from her.

Cat swallowed his nut and eyed him, grinning.

"I love you, Savage." She climbed out of the bed and approached him slowly. "You love me, Lil Boy?" She asked, grabbing his chain. "Tell me!" She grabbed his dick and jerked it. Savage looked at her and grinned. "Tell me, Savage," she cried, jerking his dick even faster. Cat opened her pussy lips and slid his dick up and down her moist slit while gazing into his eyes. "Tell me!" She moaned, biting her bottom lip, rubbing his dick faster up and down her clit. Cat's pussy was soaking wet. Savage felt his nut coming and grabbed her, ready to fuck.

Cat stopped him and let his dick go and walked to the bed. Laying on her back, she opened her legs, and finger-fucked herself.

"Tell me you love me," she moaned, sliding two fingers in and out of her pussy. Savage's dick was rock hard as he walked to her. "Tell me," Cat looked into his eyes, covering her pussy with her hands. "No pussy till you tell me." She grinned, looking sexy as shit, as she slid three fingers in and out her pussy. "Ohhh, Savageeee," she moaned, looking at Savage, with pussy juice dripping down her thighs.

Savage's dick was super hard. "I love you," he said. He was just trying to fuck.

Cat smiled and put her legs in a wide V. "Fuck me."

Savage climbed between her legs, and slid in her hot, moist cave. Pinning her legs behind her ears, he fucked the shit out of her.

"You want to play?" Savage said through clenched teeth, slamming his dick in and out of her pussy. "Say, I'm sorry!" he ordered, grinding in her pussy, hard, hitting all her walls.

"I'm…ohhh, Savage, you fucking me so gooddd," she whimpered, loving his dick as he put it in her stomach.

"Say it," Savage demanded, feeling his nut coming.

"I'mm… ahhh… I'm sorryyyyy!" Cat screamed and came. Savage came at the same time and collapsed on her, nutting all in her pussy. "I love you, Lil Boy," she confessed, kissing him all over his face and lips.

Savage slid out of her pussy and stood up with his dick coated white. Cat got up, grabbed his hand, and walked him to the shower. They washed up, fucked, and washed up again.

They hopped out the shower and got dressed. Cat put on an all-black Chanel sundress that showed off all of her curves and an all-black thong, with some red bottom heels.

Savage threw on a hittin' ass Dior sweat suit, with the Yeezy boost sneakers. He put his flats in his ears, his Savage shit chain around his neck, and his F&N in his pocket.

"Let's go eat first, then hit Tyson 2," Savage stated while watching Cat put 25 bands in her Chanel bag.

"Alright, baby." Cat threw on her Chanel shades and followed Savage out the apartment.

Savage had his hand on the F&N, finger on the trigger. He knew that had a mask on last night's move, but fuck that, he wasn't doing no lacking. Outside, he looked around and saw yellow tape on the ground in front of 1105 but it was a ghost town.

"When you get this car, boo?" Cat asked as they hopped in the car.

"None of yours." Savage sat in the driver seat, put his F&N on his lap and checked the mirrors.

"Savage, don't get smacked. Smart ass!" Cat rolled her eyes and grabbed the aux cord to hook up her phone.

"Fuck is you doin', Moe?" Savage asked, looking at Cat like she was crazy.

"Savage, Boy," Cat waved him off and cut on Megan the Stallion.

"I ain't listenin' to this shit all day," Savage told her as he pulled off.

Cat didn't pay him any mind; she glanced at him and danced as she cut the music up.

SIX
FREAKY
HUNTWOOD - 1:00 P.M

RING, *Ring, Ring*

"Yeah?" Freaky slurred as he answered the phone.

"I'ma pull up in 10 minutes," Nook said and hung up.

Freaky sat up on the couch and looked around his one-bedroom apartment. He was still tired because he didn't get in the house until six in the morning. Getting off the couch, he walked to the window, and peeked out the blinds to check his surroundings.

He came up on 10 bands and two dogs from the lick Nook put him on, and on the table, he already had Nook's cut in a bag waiting on him: $3500 and a Springfield 9. Freaky was keeping $6500 and the 5th. He walked to his room, put the Taurus 9 in his sweatpants pocket, threw on a T-shirt and shoes, brushed his teeth, and was about to twist up his first J of the day when his phone rang. He answered on the first ring.

"I'm out front," Nook said and hung up.

Freaky walked into the living room, grabbed the bag off the table, walked to the window, and saw Nook sitting in his Maxima. He put his hand in his pocket around the Taurus and stepped out of his apartment. He smelled gas as soon as he stepped in the hallway and saw two young girls sitting on the steps smoking.

"Aye, Boy," one girl called as Freaky walked pass.

Paying them no mind, he looked out the hallway door, and went to step out when he heard one of the girls say, "He scared of this pussy!"

They both giggled.

"Fast ass," Freaky said, smiling as he stepped out of the building. The sun was shining, and kids were running up and down the block. Freaky nodded to a few people posted up and walked to Nook's Maxima.

"Here, Moe." Freaky handed Nook the bag through the window. Freaky's hand was still in his pocket, on the Taurus, eyes on his surroundings as he talked to Nook.

"I got something else lined up. I'ma hit you later. Oh yeah, the nigga you hit on a shit bag," Nook informed, laughing. He dapped Freaky up and pulled off.

Freaky walked back to the building, stepped in, and looked at the two young girls. Their eyes were low and red. Both of them had on little skirts and wore their hair in ponytails. The bold one from earlier that spoke out was brown skinned, the other was a redbone. Both of them were cute but you could tell they were babies.

"What was you sayin'?" Freaky asked, grinning as he walked up to the one that was talking.

She blushed. Her friend was smiling from ear-to-ear.

"Fire up. Where the weed at?" The brown-skinned one asked, looking at Freaky and rubbing her thighs together.

"Come on." Freaky looked around before grabbing both their hands and walking to his apartment.

SAVAGE - 2:50 P.M

"Baby, you like these?" Cat asked, showing Savage a hitting ass Moncler sweater and some Balenciaga boots.

"Yeah, get them. I'm bout to go to the jewelry store really quick," he told her and went in her purse and grabbed 10 bands.

Cat gave him a kiss and watched as he walked out of Saks. Savage nodded to a few girls looking his way as he walked in the jewelry store.

The jeweler saw Savage walk into the store and fixed her titties in her blouse. Making sure they were sitting up, she watched him look around. *Got damn this guy is fine.*

"Hi, how are you doing today, sir. My name is Jessica. Need any help today?" She walked around the counter and stood right in front of Savage, pushing her titties out.

Jessica was white with blond hair and blue-eyes. She had big titties, a slim, tight, sexy body with a nice little ass. She also had a nasty look about her that you just knew she'd suck the shit out a dick and let you fuck her in every hole.

"Yeah, you could help me. I'm Savage." Savage shook her hand with a grin, dick getting hard as he looked from her lips to her titties. "You could help me by givin' me your number, and I want to buy that

Tag Huer behind the glass." Savage looked into her eyes as she let his hand go, smiling. Her pussy was dripping wet, nipples hard, and her face was red as she walked back behind the counter.

"I think I can help you with both." She grabbed the watch from behind the glass.

Savage put his phone on the counter, grabbed the watch, put it on his wrist, and watched Jessica put her number in his phone.

"That costs $5000, and the good pussy is free. I'll be waiting on your call. I get off work at 6 tonight."

Savage put 5 bands on the counter. "I'ma call," he told her, putting his watch on and walking out of the store.

"I can tell he got a big dick," Jessica said to herself, horny as shit as she watched Savage walk out of the store.

———

Savage stopped at the door when he saw Cat smiling all up in some tall, brown-skinned guy's face. The tall dude was foreign down, wrist and neck iced out. He looked sweet. You could smell the money on the nigga. Savage just fell back and watched. He really wanted to walk up and smack the shit out of Cat, rob, and strip the nigga she was talking to ass naked. What really hurt was watching Cat give the nigga her number and a kiss on the lips. Savage knew Cat did her but to see it up close threw him off.

He waited until the dude walked off and approached like he hadn't seen anything. Cat's hands were full of bags. She smiled when Savage walked up looking at his watch.

"I like that Boo," she complimented and stood on her tiptoes to kiss him on his lips.

Thot ass bitch, Savage thought to himself as he grabbed some bags.

Cat grabbed his free hand as they walked out of the mall. They hopped in the Charger and Savage saw the dude Cat was talking to pull off in an all-white 550 Benz.

"I love you so much, Lil Boy," Cat said, watching Savage as he started the car. Savage grabbed the F&N from under his seat and sat it on his lap. "I said I love you, Savage!" Savage just looked at her like she was stupid. "Why you acting all shady and shit, Savage. Uggh!" She yelled, looking in his face.

Savage turned his head to the road and pulled off. Cat smacked the F&N on the floor and started grabbing at his pants.

"Watch out!" Savage smacked her hands.

"Move!" She smacked his hands, pulled his dick out of his pants, and put it in her mouth. As soon as Cat put his dick in her mouth Savage just laid back and cruised through the city.

Cat sucked him dry. "I'm going always love you no matter what. You belong to me," she declared, kissing his cheek when he pulled in front of her building. Cat grabbed her bags and hopped out of the car thinking about the nigga she met in the mall as she walked into her building.

Savage pulled off. Neither of them peeped Black and Floyd sitting in the truck watching them. Black just nodded, plotting, thinking, *I got you Cash. I'ma crush both of 'em.*

SEVEN
SAVAGE

CHOPPER CITY - 5:00 P.M.

SAVAGE PULLED up to Chopper City and parked two buildings down from Aunt J's building. He put the F&N in his sweatpants and hopped out the Charger. He walked up the block and saw a police cruiser riding his way. *Damn*, he thought to himself.

"Aye, Young Savage. Did you rob or kill anyone today?" Officer Gram asked from the passenger seat of the cruiser.

Savage didn't respond. He already had his mind made up, if they told him to stop... he was breaking. He wasn't getting caught with a gun on him.

"Hold fast real quick, Savage. What's that lump in your pocket?" Officer Gram asked, seeing a lump every time Savage walked.

"Hold up," Savage said and took off running.

"Stop! Call backup. Stop!" Officer Gram yelled as he jumped out of the cruiser.

Savage ran full speed up Greenway, looking over his shoulder and seeing Gram behind him. He heard the sirens as he cut through Unity's parking lot.

"Freeze now!" Officer Gram yelled trying to catch Savage.

As Savage ran down the hill, he saw a police cruiser speeding his way. Cutting through a house, he hopped a fence, and ran up the alley.

He looked over his shoulder and saw Gram trying to hop the fence. Breaking out of the alley, he ran up 16th St., and heard sirens as he ran into building 605. The sirens were blasting as he ran up the hallway steps. His heart was drumming in his chest as he banged on the door of apartment four, with his face watching the hallway door.

When the apartment door opened, Savage ran in and laid straight on the floor, tired and breathing hard.

"Boy, you always getting in trouble," Dawn stated. She smiled as she stood in front of Savage in a pair of black booty shorts and a tank top on.

Savage laid out on the floor trying to catch his breath. He dug in his pocket and pulled out a stack, counting out $600.

"Get some gas and food. I'm cooling up here today," Savage told her, holding out the money.

Dawn walked up and made sure he saw her phat ass pussy print as she grabbed the money out of his hand.

"I'm a fuck your lil ass today, too," Savage promised. He watched Dawn walk to her room, ass jiggling in her boy-shorts.

Dawn smiled, feeling herself getting wet.

Savage took the F&N out of his pocket, and laid it on his chest thinking, *I ain't getting caught or throwing no dogs away, fuck that!*

CAT - 6:40 P.M

"I'm a savage, classy, bougie, ratchet," Cat rapped to Megan Thee Stallion while standing in front of her full-length mirror in a red thong and a pair of red bottom heels. "'Bitch, what's happenin'?'" She rapped, clapping her ass when she heard a knock on the door "What? What? What?" She shouted and stomped to the door, ass clapping with each step she took. She looked out the peephole, sucked her teeth and snatched the door open. "What, bitch?!"

"Ugh, bitch, put some fucking clothes on," Bubbles said, looking her up and down as she stepped into the house in a see-through one piece.

Bubbles was a 25-year-old, 5'3, 130-pound redbone. Tatted-up with roses all over her body, she was bad. She resembled Karrueche Tran with long jet-black dreads that hung to her ass. Her body was hitting. Plump ass, nice round titties, feet a torch, and she had a walk that made you want to fuck on sight.

"Bitch, this is my house." Cat smiled as she shut and locked the door. "You just mad your ass don't move like this." Cat walked in front of Bubbles throwing her ass in a circle.

Bubbles grinned and followed Cat into her room.

"Where mine?" Bubbles asked pouting, peeking around Cat's room at all the Saks 5th bags everywhere.

Cat busted out laughing, shaking her head. "Bitch you know I got you something, crybaby ass." Cat was still laughing as she walked to the closet and grabbed a shoebox. "Here, crybaby." Cat handed Bubbles the box.

Bubbles grabbed the shoebox and sat on the bed smiling ear-to-ear as she opened the box to see the heels she'd been wanting for the last six months. "Thank you, Cat," Bubbles screeched, kicking off her heels and trying on the new ones.

"Girl, don't thank me," Cat replied, sitting down on the bed and grabbing some sheets and gas off her dresser. "Thank Savage!"

"Girl, what's up with Savage anyway? His bad ass so cute and he be on his shit. You need to share," Bubbles said as she stood up and walked around in her new heels.

Cat looked at Bubbles with fire in her eyes and heatedly said, "Bitch, don't play with me. He's off limits, period!" Cat asserted and fired up her J.

"Girl, why you so serious. I was just playing," Bubbles lied, rolling her eyes at Cat.

Bubbles had been on Savage's line for years but had never been able to catch him dolo. She loved everything about him. Every time she got around him her pussy got wet.

"Anyway," Cat changed the subject, "guess who's coming to get me tonight?" She grinned as she hit her J.

"Who, bitch? You know I'm not good at this guessing and shit."

"V, bitch!" Cat shrieked as she put the J in the ashtray. Cat was high off that good cookie. The weed had her horny.

"V from uptown, with the 550?" Bubbles asked.

"Yes him," Cat said as she spread her legs open in front of her.

"Girl, you pressed," Bubbles said, looking at Cat. "Fuck is your nasty ass doing?" Bubbles asked, seeing the front of Cat's thong soaking wet.

Cat looked at her laughing. "You want to see why these niggas be going crazy over this pussy?" Cat asked, looking Bubbles in her eyes.

"Fuck no!" Bubbles denounced, laughing. "Anyway, the reason I came over is because," she stood up from the bed and watched as Cat took off her thong, "I started fucking with this VA nigga. He was cool at first, then he started doing too much. Showing off his money, bragging, a lot of clown shit." As she spoke, Bubbles continued watching Cat as she spread her legs and rubbed her fingers up and down her slit. Bubbles felt herself getting horny from watching. "I saw his clown ass count 50 bands in my face. Can you get Savage to rob him for me please?" She asked, pouting as she looked at Cat's pussy juice dripping down her leg.

"Bitch, fuck no!" Cat yelled, sitting up and eyeing Bubbles like she was stupid.

"Please Cat. I need the money," Bubbles pleaded.

Cat shook her head. "Bitch, it better be 50, too. I need 5 bands and my pussy licked," Cat stipulated, rolling her eyes, and grabbing her phone off the dresser.

Dialing Savage's number, Cat laid back on the bed, spread her legs, and opened her pussy lips. Bubbles shook her head while walking up to her. Getting comfortable in between her legs, she began to lick her pussy.

———

"Boy, you not all that," Dawn said, smiling from ear-to-ear sitting on Savage's lap with her legs wrapped around his waist, playing with his chain.

"Girl, you know you on his dick. Look at you," Mya said, laughing as she ate a slice of pizza.

"And so what? Who gon' check me?" Dawn asked, rolling her eyes and kissing Savage's neck.

"Where Freaky at?" Mya asked when Savage's phone rang.

"Get that," Savage told her and smacked Dawn on her ass. She rolled her eyes, got up, and handed him his phone then sat back on his lap. Mya just laughed as she watched Savage answer his phone.

"Yeah?"

"Hey, baby," Cat greeted in a light moan, pushing Bubble's face further into her pussy. "Bubbles got something she want to holla at you about." Cat pulled Bubble's head from her pussy. It was feeling too good, and she didn't want Savage to hear her moaning.

Bubbles grinned with pussy juice all over her face.

"She wants you to meet her at the club tonight around 1:00a.m. It's about some money."

"Alright, tell her I'll be there."

"Alright baby. I love you, Savage."

"Love you, too," Savage stated and hung up.

"Who was that, your bitch?" Dawn asked as Savage's hand slid up her thigh.

"Yeah," he said, rubbing her phat pussy through her boy shorts.

"Heee said okayyyy," Cat moaned as Bubbles sucked her clit. Bubbles pushed Cat's legs behind her head and licked from her pussy to her ass. She was tongue fucking her hole, sliding her tongue back to her pussy. "Yesss," Cat moaned with her eyes closed, grinding on Bubbles' face.

EIGHT
SAVAGE - CHOPPER CITY

"OHHHH, SAVAGE... I'M COMING, YESSSS," Dawn screamed as Savage pinned her legs behind her head and jumped in and out of her pussy.

All you heard was skin slapping as Savage fucked the shit out of her.

"Y'all so fucking nasty," Mya let out as she watched from the couch she sat on. Her pussy was soaked. She wanted to get fucked.

"Take it, take this dick!" Savage commanded through clenched teeth as he grinded in her, pulling his dick to the tip of her pussy, then slamming it back deep in her. Every time Savage slid his dick out, it was coated white with her juices.

"Ahhh, Ohh, Savage cum in this pussy, cum in meee!" Dawn screamed with her legs in a wide V. She pulled Savage deep into her, holding his back as she came all over his dick.

Savage was still grinding as he grabbed her arms and put them behind her head while he was crushing her pussy.

"Savage, I'm done, shittt, I'm done," she moaned, closing her eyes and cumming again.

"Shit!" He yelled as he came all over her pussy and stomach. Savage was breathing hard as he laid back on the couch and caught his breath.

Dawn was still shaking, creamy cum pouring out of her pussy with her eyes closed, feeling good as shit.

"Ugh! Y'all so nasty." Mya got up from the couch and looked at Savage's dick as she made her way to the bathroom.

She walked in, shut the door behind her and took off her pants. Putting her back against the wall, she rubbed her nipples with one hand, and reached down to pull her thong to the side with the other before licking her finger and massaging her clit. She put her legs in the air, took off her thong, then closed her eyes and thought about Savage. Sliding two fingers in and out of her pussy, she bit her lip and let her head fall back.

"Fuck me!" she moaned, fingering herself faster, pussy juice dripping down her thighs. "Savage, Ohhh Savage," she moaned in a whisper, squeezing her eyes closed as she came all over her fingers. She laid there for a second smiling, got up, and washed her hands and pussy.

Putting her sweats back on, she threw her thong in the bottom of Dawn's dirty clothes bin and walked out of the bathroom.

Savage was sitting on the couch twisting up while Dawn was getting off the floor smiling.

"Let me go take a shower real quick," Dawn said, walking past Mya in just her T-shirt with her boy shorts in her hand.

"Why y'all so nasty?" Mya asked, walking past Savage.

Savage got up, grabbed Mya by the arm, pulled her sweatpants down to her ankles, bent her over the arm of the couch, and slid in her pussy.

"Uhnnnn!" she moaned as Savage held her waist and drilled her pussy. She was throwing her ass back at him, biting her lip to keep from moaning too loud as the shower's water ran. "Savage faster, hit this pussy faster," she moaned, feeling the pressure building.

Savage was pounding her, slamming his dick in and out of her pussy.

This pussy good as shit, he thought.

"I'm cumming. It feels so good Savageee!" Mya cried tears of joy as she came all over his dick.

Savage was still hitting her pussy at an angle. He pulled out and shot nut all over Mya's ass, smacking his dick on her ass cheeks, just as the shower cut off.

Savage put his dick in his pants, sat on the couch, and fired up a J.

Mya pulled up her sweats and walked to the kitchen just as Dawn stepped out of the bathroom in some little ass shorts and a baby white T-shirt.

Dawn walked straight into the living room. The weed covered up the sex smell.

Mya slid out of the kitchen and walked into the bathroom to clean herself up.

That dick was good, she thought.

"Savage, I'm mad at you," Dawn said as she sat on the couch beside him and put her legs across his lap.

"Why'?" he asked, grinning at her, blowing smoke in the air.

"Why didn't you nut in me?"

"What?" Savage said and busted out laughing.

"I'm not fucking laughing," she said, punching him in his chest and snatching the J out of his hand. Dawn rolled her eyes, and hit the J. "You know Smoke got killed last night."

"Killed?!" Savage replied with his mind going straight to Freaky.

"Yeah," Mya said, walking in the living room. "Greg got locked up this morning, but I heard him and Dog talking this morning. They said Freaky kilt him because Smoke's body was laid out beside Freaky's 650," Mya relayed as she sat on the edge of the couch.

Dawn passed her the J.

"Where Dog at?" Savage asked, grabbing his phone. *I got to kill this nigga Dog, ASAP!*

"I ain't see him today," Dawn watched Savage dial a number.

He stood up, walking back and forth.

———

"Open your legs a lil wider," Freaky told Pam. He was sitting on the couch beside her, sliding his finger in and out of her pussy.

"Ouuu," she moaned as she laid back on the couch, spreading her legs wider. Her skirt was raised up to her hips.

Pam, the young girl doing the talking earlier, was 14, as was her friend Jaz. Freaky had smoked an ounce of cookie with them. Jaz was too high and went to sleep. Freaky ate Pam's pussy, tongue fucking her ass all day, turning her young ass out.

"Shhhhh," he whispered as he pulled out his dick and climbed between Pam's legs, sliding in her pussy.

"Ahhh," Pam moaned, nutting as Freaky slid in her deeper, slow stroking her young pussy. Pam loved that it filled her whole pussy. She opened her legs wider and pulled Freaky in her deeper. "Yesssss!" She cried out, closing her eyes. Freaky was so focused on fucking Pam, he didn't hear his phone ring.

———

"Fuck this wild ass nigga at?" Savage said to himself, listening to the phone going to voicemail for the third time. He shook his head and put his phone in his pocket. "I'm bout to slide. I'll be back later."

"Where you going?" Dawn yelled, catching an attitude.

"I'll be back later," he repeated, putting the F&N in his pocket.

"Whatever," Dawn chided, pouting and crossing her arms over her chest looking at him.

Savage laughed. "Alright Mya," he said and walked out of the apartment.

"You on Savage's dick, girl," Mya affirmed, looking at Dawn, laughing.

"Girl, he up, cute, turned up, and that dick like that. That's my dude," Dawn admitted as she walked to the window and watched Savage walk up the block.

That dick is good, Mya said to herself, laying back on the couch high as shit.

Savage made it to his car, hopped in, and pulled off thinking about Dog. He needed to find out where he was and crush him before he could catch him or Freaky lacking.

———

If Savage would have waited two more minutes, he would have seen Dog walking out of his building. Dog had just got finished getting his dick sucked by Aunt J. Aunt J didn't have any money and was geeking for a hit. Plus, after that night with Freaky, she was back to her old ways. Even though she used to trick to get a hit, she loved the feeling of sucking dick and getting fucked while she was high. Dog taped the whole thing, smiling as he walked up the block. Even as he sinned God had been on his side.

NINE

BIG MIKE - 11:50 P.M

BIG MIKE WAS PACING his office floor after he got off the phone with the Made Man. The Made Man needed someone dead tonight, ASAP! The Made Man was in the middle of a big drug conspiracy case and felt he couldn't trust anybody. He knew Big Mike was a stand-up man and could get things done, so he paid him a visit. The Made Man showed up with 70 thousand cash and told Big Mike that he needed his assistance. Even though Mike wasn't in the streets anymore, he owed this man. Plus, he knew the Made Man was a stand-up man, too.

Big Mike took the money and told him that he was on top of it and let his mind roam. The first people he thought of for the job was Savage and Freaky. Big Mike grabbed his phone thinking, *I'ma keep 20. I know slim gon' work the nigga for 50.*

Big Mike dialed Freaky's number, praying he answered.

———

"Damn, this pussy good," Freaky whispered in Pam's ear, grinding in her tight, wet pussy. Freaky slid as deep as he could go and came all in her pussy. He kissed her lips and pulled his dick out of her.

Pam just laid there, legs cocked open, feeling good. Coming down from orgasmic bliss, she watched Freaky with love in her eyes.

Jaz lay on the floor sleep with her skirt up over her ass, showing her little ass cheeks and pink panties. Freaky pulled her panties to the side and slid a finger in and out of her young pussy. Jaz moaned as he slid in her slowly when his phone rang.

He pulled his finger out and she looked at him smiling. Freaky sucked her juices off his finger and walked to his pants ass naked, dick swinging.

Jaz and Pam were looking at each other, cheesing as Freaky answered his phone.

"Freaky?" Mike called, still pacing, phone glued to his ear.

"What's up?" Freaky greeted, walking to Jaz and putting his dick in her face. Jaz giggled with a shy look on her face as she grabbed his dick and put it in her mouth.

"Look, I'ma cut straight to the chase. I got 50 thousand right here for you, but I need this shit done tonight!" Big Mike said with urgency in his voice. He was sitting at his desk looking at the bag of money.

"Where you at?" Freaky asked, making Jaz stop. He pulled his dick out of her mouth.

"At the office. This shit needs to be done ASAP!" Big Mike stressed.

"I'm on my way," Freaky confirmed before hanging up and putting on his clothes.

Jaz and Pam watched him run to his room.

Freaky lifted his bed, grabbed his 357, and put it on his hip. He grabbed 400 dollars and walked in the living room. He gave Pam and Jaz 200 apiece and kissed both of them on their lips.

"I'll be back," Freaky said and jogged out of the apartment.

"That's my dude!" Pam yelled, smiling as she looked at Jaz.

Jaz looked at the *money. None of my boyfriend's give me money.*

Pam began to tell Jaz about her and Freaky's sexcapades.

"I can't wait til he fuck me," Jaz told Pam as she listened to Pam give her the details.

———

Freaky did the dash, running lights with 50 bands on his mind. He pulled up to Mike's car lot, parked, hopped out, and walked to Mike's office.

Big Mike watched Freaky from when he first made the turn up the block. He had cameras stashed all over the place and was the only one that knew where they were. He stayed on point. It was one of the many ways he had managed to stay around so long.

Freaky walked in the office, and Big Mike cut straight to the point. "The nigga's name is Johnny," Big Mike pulled out a picture and held it up. "He needs to be dead before 4:00 am." Big Mike looked at his watch. "He owns a bar on 8th and H street called *Drinks*. He's there now. This 50 right here." Big Mike opened the bag to show Freaky stacks of 50s and 100s.

"If you handle this right, slim, it's going to be plenty more work for you. I know you and Savage be doing y'all, but this shit right here is the big leagues," Big Mike said, looking in his eyes.

He right, 50 bands to spank a nigga, Freaky thought. *I been doing that shit for free for years.*

Freaky grabbed the picture and left out, jogging to his car.

Big Mike sat in his chair and laid back, watching Freaky pull off. He smiled. *I'm back in this shit, putting a plan together.* He thought about how much he was going to be comfortable with before he made his exit yet again.

"Nothing lasts forever!" He said, thinking out loud.

———

Freaky cruised up 8th street looking for a bar called *Drinks*. He saw the bar's sign on the corner on the same street that *Horse and Dickey's* was on, across the street from the *Auto Zone*. Freaky parked on a side street, looked at the picture one more time, hopped out the car and walked to the bar.

When he walked in the bar, he looked around and saw people sitting at tables, talking and drinking. The music played as Freaky scanned the bar looking for Johnny. He walked up to the bar, and a tall, pretty face white woman with red hair walked up to him and asked what he was having.

"I'm new here. Get me something good." Freaky looked around for Johnny.

"Here you go, honey." The bartender sat a glass in front of him.

Freaky took a sip, cleared his throat and held up the glass. "What's this?"

"Deleón."

Freaky smiled. "Oh, you know something."

The bartender laughed. "I know a street guy or two."

"How you know I'm street?" Freaky sat the glass down and folded his arms, still smiling.

She shrugged. "I don't. You didn't exactly peg me as the whisky type either, though."

"Fair enough." Freaky grabbed the glass and held her gaze as he took another swallow. He looked around behind himself and feigned confusion. "Where's Johnny? He tells me to show up to check out his bar and he's not here."

"Oh, Johnny," she blushed. "You must be the guy he's supposed to be meeting. I thought he left to get you. He just stepped out. Be back in a sec, I guess. This bar is his baby. He's always on the floor showing love." She exhaled heavy and glanced over the bar in admiration. "I love this place." Another customer sat at the bar down the line and flagged her over. "Oh! I gotta get this."

Freaky gave a curt nod, and the bartender scurried off. Taking another sip of his drink, he looked towards the door just as Johnny entered, talking with another guy.

Bingo! Taking a final sip, Freaky sat his glass on the counter. Getting up, he walked slowly by them, watching Johnny and the other guy take a seat at the bar. Freaky walked out and jogged to the gas station. He bought a ski mask, rolled it on his head, and grabbed the .357 as he walked back to the bar with 50 bands on his mind.

"Johnny." The bartender sat his favorite drink in front of him.

She greeted his friend, looked at Johnny's face and saw stress. She knew about the case he was facing but didn't know how serious it was. She didn't know the reason he was stressed was because he was about to tell on people he grew up with. She was about to tell him about the guy that came in earlier asking about him when she saw a masked man running in the bar. Her eyes grew big, Johnny saw the look on her face and turned.

Boom!

The shot hit him in his chest, and his eyes were wide with fear as he crumbled to the ground sending the bar into an uproar. Everyone was screaming, running, and trying to get away. The guy Johnny was with took off for the door. Freaky ran over to Johnny, stood over him and emptied the clip into his body to make sure he was dead.

The bartender was in shock. Her face was now pale as she watched Freaky frozen in fear. He up the dog, shot her, and ran out the bar to his car. Hopping in, he smashed out on the way to collect his ends.

The bitch coulda been a witness later. I ain't takin' no chances, he said to himself. "Fuck that!"

TEN
SAVAGE
NEW YORK AVE. - 12:20 P.M.

SAVAGE PULLED up to Exotics Strip club, parked, and sat in the car looking around, seeing all types of exotic cars in the parking lot. He watched people walk in the club with all types of jewelry on. One dude hopped out an Audi with a bust down on his wrist. Savage knew if he bagged him, he'd come up on at least 15 to 20 bands easy, and that was just off the watch. He pulled out his phone and looked at him and Freaky's conversation thread. Still no reply.

He shook his head. *Ain't nothin' wrong with this nigga,* he thought, trying to convince himself that Freaky was okay. *Lame ass could at least hit back. Probably trippin' with some bitches somewhere.* He kept telling himself that if Freaky was dead or in jail he would know by now. Word on the curbs of D.C spread fast. Savage took a deep breath an exhaled, eying the guy who had hopped out the Audi with the bust down on his wrist.

I should say fuck Bubbles, wait right here, and follow one of these sweet ass niggas home, he said to himself as he hopped out of his Charger. Savage looked around the parking lot, stuffed the F&N in his pocket, and walked to the club.

The music was blasting, and bad bitches were walking in and out the club as Savage walked to cut the line. He paid a bouncer a band to let him in with the dog and another $100 to a sexy ass native looking stripper sitting at the door. She stamped his hand, blew him a kiss, and watched him walk in. Savage entered and looked around. Club lights flashed off the walls, bounced off people's jewelry, and made the diamonds glow and dance in the dark.

All you saw was bad bitches, none under a 9, walking around in nothing but heels and it was all types of flavors to pick from. The club was big. It had two levels, upstairs was strictly V.I.P. They also had V.I.P. rooms if you were trying to fuck. It was $200 for an hour plus what the strippers wanted. Downstairs had three stages in the middle of the room, two bars, one as soon as you walked in and another one right next to the steps leading to the V.I.P. section. It had chairs, couches, and tables all over the room. They served nothing but Rosé, Cîroc, and Ace of Spades.

The owner of the club was an old head named Tone. Word on the streets, he was worth a couple million. He owned several car lots, stores, strip clubs, and was flooding the city with the best dope. He moved like a ghost. Very few people had ever saw his face. The streets only heard his name, and it was always good things that came behind it.

"Hey, cutie," a stripper called, walking up to Savage. She grabbed his dick through his pants and rubbed it as she whispered in his ear. "You cute *and* this dick big. Why don't you let me make you happy?" Grabbing his hand, she slid it up and down her wet slit.

Savage stepped back, looked at her, pulled out his knot, and handed her a hunnid. "I'm on something."

"Thank you. Maybe next time, Daddy." She kissed his cheek and walked off, ass clapping as she went.

Damn, she phat, Savage thought, watching her ass as he walked to a table in the back of the club. He always positioned himself to where he could see the whole club and the front door.

He scanned the club and saw three dudes sitting in the V.I.P. section. You could see their neck, wrist, and ears glowing as they drank Ace out the bottle and threw 100s at the strippers. They were all over them.

I might trunk me a nigga tonight, Savage thought as he watched them until a waitress walked up and caught his attention.

"Hi, Sexy. Would you like a drink?" She asked, standing there in a little ass skirt that stopped at the top of her thighs. Her pretty brown ass cheeks were sticking out the bottom and glitter covered her nipples. She was tall and petite, and reminded him of Drea off the reality show, *Basketball Wives.*

"Yeah," Savage said, looking her up and down, pulling out a knot. "Get me 2 bottles of Rosé, and $1000 in ones. You keep the change, but you gotta let me see that pretty pussy from the back." He handed her two bands.

She grabbed the money, bit her bottom lip, turned, bent over, and lifted up her skirt to show Savage her pretty pussy. She smiled over her shoulder at him and walked off.

"You want a dance?" A sexy ass stripper had approached Savage's table. He caught her from his peripheral but hadn't been alarmed due to her bein' a woman.

"Maybe next time, I'm on something tonight," he said, looking at her body.

"Ok, sexy. I'm a hold you to that." She winked and walked off.

The waitress came back, sat the bottles on his table, and gave him the money. She leaned over and whispered in Savage's ear, putting her titties in his face.

"I'm Star." Grabbing his face, she kissed him on the lips and was about to sit down when Bubbles walked up and grabbed her arm.

"He's with me," Bubbles said, looking Star up and down with that, *I'll fuck you up* look.

"Bye Sexy," Star bidded and walked off.

"You sure having fun, ain't you?" Bubbles asked, standing with her pussy right in Savage's face.

Savage laughed and slid a finger up and down her slit. He grabbed his bottle of Rosé and took a sip. Bubbles had her dreads tied in a bun on the top of her head, showing off her pretty face. Her phat pussy was sitting high, shaved with her phat clit peeking through the lips. She stood tall in her heels, looking good.

"Hi, Savage," she greeted and tried to sit on his lap, but Savage grabbed her waist.

"I got the dog on me."

Bubbles smiled and sat next to him, putting one leg on the couch, making sure he could see her pussy.

Savage took a sip of his drink. *This bitch phat.*

"What's up?" He asked, looking at her pussy.

"You can touch her." Bubbles grinned. "I got a friend name Coo," she said, looking in Savage's eyes, spreading her legs, letting him slide a finger in and out of her pussy. "He's a clown." Bubbles moaned, rotated her hips, and let Savage slide a third finger in and out of her. Savage's dick was hard watching Bubbles moan, making sexy fuck faces. He wanted to fuck.

"Savageee," she cried. "Can I have that dick pleaseeee?" She asked, cumming all over his fingers.

Savage pulled his fingers out of her pussy. She grabbed them and sucked the juices off, looking in his eyes.

"What's up with the nigga?"

"I watched him count 50 thousand in my face two days ago. He act like he's a real nigga. I see right through that shit."

"50 bands?" Savage asked, making sure he heard her correctly.

"50," she verified.

"You know where he lives?" Savage said, wanting that 50.

"Hell yeah. He on my line. I know all about his clown ass," Bubbles said, rolling her eyes. "He's coming to get me at 2 am."

"Bet! Text me the address, ASAP!" Savage looked at his watch, seeing it was 1:20 am. "Who them niggas up there purping and shit?" Savage nodded towards the V.I.P. section.

"That's," she pointed, "Claw, Keith, and Boosie. They from up Clay Terrace. Them niggas getting money and all of them want a taste of this pussy," she added, already knowing what type of time he was on.

"Alright, hurry up and text the address." Savage stood up and drank the rest of his drink. He counted off 200 ones from the stack. "That's you," he said to Bubbles, nodding to the $800 and walked off.

Bubbles just sat there watching Savage, loving his swag. *I got to have him.* Getting up, she grabbed the money and walked to the locker room.

Star was watching Savage the whole time he was at the table with Bubbles. She didn't know what it was, but she liked him and smiled as she watched him walk her way.

"Aye, Star," he called, walking to the bar.

"What's up, boo?" She greeted, blushing.

"They call me Savage. Next time I run into you... you got to let me know why they call you Star," he smiled and handed her the $200. Then, he turned and walked out of the club.

Star's gaze followed him. *Fuck Bubbles! Next time I see him, he's mine.*

––––––––

Bubbles walked in the locker room and headed to her locker.

"Bitch, who was that nigga?" China asked, walking up to Bubbles, watching as Bubbles put her money in her bag and grab her phone texting.

"Nobody, a trick," Bubbles said as she texted Savage the address.

"Bitch, not with his fingers all in your pussy and you sucking his fingers and shit."

China was thick as shit. A tall Amazon, bad bitch with chinky eyes. That's why they called her China. She was a nosey snake ass bitch, and everybody knew not to tell her shit.

"Girl." Bubbles rolled her eyes, locked her locker, and walked back to the main room.

"Bitch, fuck you then!" China yelled, watching Bubbles walk away with hate in her eyes.

––––––––

Coo was sitting in his green Range Rover at 2am on the dot. *Damn, this bitch Bubbles like that,* Coo thought as he watched Bubbles step out of the club in a pair of black leggings. Her dreads hung by her waist. Her phat pussy print was on display, ass jiggling as she walked to the truck and climbed in.

"Hey, Daddy," she greeted, kissing Coo on his cheek as he pulled off.

Coo stuck his hand between her thighs, rubbing her pussy through the fabric. Bubbles spread her legs, letting him get more access. She wanted him to be comfortable, but on the inside, she hated his touch.

"I had a good day, made a nice bankroll," Coo bragged as he hit I-95.

When they pulled up to his apartment, Coo was geeking. Bubbles had been jerking and sucking his dick, teasing him the whole ride. Coo was ready to fuck. They got out and headed to his spot. He didn't peep someone walk pass his truck as he walked up to the building.

"I'ma fuck the shit out of you." Coo grabbed Bubble's ass as they walked in his building.

Coo wasn't pay attention to someone walking down the hallway steps, as he put his key in the door. Savage put the F&N to the back of his head.

"Don't scream," he said to Bubbles. "Open the door!"

Coo was scared to death as Savage searched him and took the dog off his hip.

Savage pushed him and Bubbles in the house. Bubbles played the scared role, pussy dripping wet watching Savage work.

"Where that shit at?" Savage asked with the F&N in Coo's face.

"I ain't sweet..."

Smack!

Savage smacked the shit out of Coo with the F&N.

"Ahhh, fuck!" Coo screamed.

Savage made Coo give him everything, then he stripped him, and left his ass naked, crying, and bleeding in front of Bubbles.

Bubbles looked at Coo crying. *This nigga a bitch!*

Despite the fact, she played the role like she cared, all the while, thinking about her cut and fucking Savage.

––––––

Bubbles caught an Uber home, texting Savage the whole ride. They met up at her house an hour later.

Coo only had 30 bands and an 8th of coke. Savage let Bubbles keep the 8th and 18 bands. He took 12 and was about to leave when Bubbles walked out of her room ass naked.

"Can I have that dick, please?" She asked, biting her bottom lip and rubbing her phat clit looking at Savage. He got ass naked and gave Bubbles everything she was looking for.

Savage went to sleep in her pussy.

This my nigga now, Bubble's thought as she laid on Savage's chest, and went to sleep with a smile on her face.

ELEVEN
CAT

TWO DAYS LATER - 7:40 A.M.

CAT SPENT the last two days sucking and fucking V crazy. She had him gone. She sucked V's dick all the way to her building and let him nut in her mouth. She swallowed everything and sucked him dry.

V told her to pack her shit, she was coming with him later, and he wanted her to stay with him all week. She gave him a kiss, hopped out of the car, and walked in her building.

V watched her the whole time, looking at her ass and grabbing his dick. As soon as she walked in her building, V pulled off. Cat didn't know Black was sitting in the building watching her. He was hip to her. Cat's life was on a countdown.

FREAKY

SIMPLE CITY – 1:40 P.M.

"Big bands nigga," Freaky said to Nook blowing gas, sitting at the table in Nook's house.

Freaky was LV down, big bust down with the VVS's busting all through his watch. He had on a big platinum Cuban link around his neck, and his ears were flooded. Freaky had the P90 Ruger with the 36 in it on him that day, 20 bands in cash in his pockets in all 100s wrapped up like it came straight out of the bank. He had the fresh fade looking sweet.

"I'm bout to pull up on Savage. We got to holla at the nigga Gucci." Freaky passed Nook the blunt just as his16-year-old sister walked past in a tank top and some pink panties stuffed up in her ass. Her pussy was phat, with little pussy hairs peeking from beneath the fabric.

Freaky looked her young ass up and down, dick getting hard as he watched her little ass cheeks move.

"Bitch, get your thot ass in the room and put on some fucking clothes!" Nook yelled, mad as shit.

"Nook, you ain't my father!" She looked at Nook with her hands on her hip, rolling her eyes.

Freaky was horny as shit looking at her little thick thighs and pussy print, and she knew he was watching.

"Fuck you, Nook!" she screamed, turned, and stomped to her room on purpose, knowing her ass was jiggling.

Damn, Freaky thought, watching as she turned the corner.

"Thot ass bitch! " Nook stressed, hitting the J hard. He wanted to get up and smack the shit out of his sister.

"I'm bout to take a piss, real quick. Call Savage and meet up with him," Freaky told Nook as he got up and walked to the bathroom.

As soon as Freaky stepped in the bathroom, Nook's sister, Jammy, opened her door wide and was standing in the doorway in just a tank top. Freaky grabbed his dick looking at her, phat hairy pussy.

"Open it," Freaky mouthed.

Jammy grinned and opened her pussy lips, showing Freaky her phat clit. Freaky was about to walk to her when Nook yelled his name. Jammy ran in her room, shut, and locked the door.

Freaky cut on the sink water and fixed his dick in his pants. He washed his hands and walked out of the bathroom, grabbing his phone out of his pocket. "I'm a catch your wild ass later." He walked out of the apartment building and called Savage.

Jammy laid on the bed with her legs in the air, fingering herself to thoughts of Freaky.

―――――

"You better nut in me, Savage," Dawn moaned as she bounced up and down on Savage's dick. Savage was sitting on the couch and Dawn was between his legs riding him, reverse cowgirl. Her feet were on the floor, while she slid up and down on his dick.

Savage was gripping her ass, opening her cheeks, watching his dick slide in and out of her pussy.

"I want you to nut in it Savageeee. Pleaseeee nut in me!" Dawn screamed, sliding all the way down on his dick, cumming.

"Watch out," Savage said about to nut, trying to push Dawn off of him.

Dawn wouldn't move as she rotated in a circle on his dick.

"Fuckkk!" Savage held her waist, grinded into her, and planted his seed. "Yo shit be geekin'." Savage laid back on the couch drained as Dawn rotated her body on his dick, getting all his nut in her.

"Boy, so what?" She said, grinning when Savage's phone rang.

"Can I answer my phone please, Ms. Dawn?" Savage asked playfully.

"Savage," she said, rolling her ass and standing up. Savage's dick slid out of her creamy pussy.

He grabbed his phone out his pocket and was about to pull up his pants when Dawn smacked his hands, got on her knees, and sucked his dick.

"Yeah, Slim," Savage greeted when he answered the phone. Then he laid back on the couch and watched Dawn as she ate his dick up.

"I'm bout to pull up on you. Where you at?" Freaky asked as he stepped out of Nook's building.

He had his hand on the Ruger, on high alert as he walked to his 650. He knew that's all they did was jack cars and rob people in Simple City. That's just how the South East got down. Freaky was worth at least 40 bands and wasn't doing any lacking as he hopped in the 650 and pulled off.

"Meet me up Dawn's joint," Savage said in a whisper as he palmed Dawn's head, fucking her mouth.

"Bet," Freaky said and hung up.

Savage dropped the phone, pushed Dawn's head all the way down on his dick, and came in her mouth.

Dawn jumped up and ran to the bathroom to spit his nut in the toilet. Savage laughed as he pulled up his pants.

"Savage, that shit ain't funny," Dawn said, walking out of the bathroom brushing her teeth.

Savage looked around the apartment, shaking his head. *It ain't shit in this joint.*

"Aye, Dawn." Savage looked at an old TV sitting on the table.

"Yes." Dawn walked up, stepped between his legs, and watched him flip through a bankroll.

"Moe, I'ma be up here and shit. You need to tighten this motherfucker up." He counted out four bands and handed it to her.

"Thank you, Savage," she said, grabbing the money and giving him a kiss on his lips.

"Shit ain't nothin'. Just tighten this motherfucker up."

"I'm on it, boo, I promise." She walked to her room counting the money. *I love this nigga.*

Savage stood up, grabbed his phone, and saw it was ringing.

"Yeah, Slim," he answered.

"I'm out front. Stop playing house, we got shit to do."

"I'm on my way." Savage hung up, grabbed his F&N and put it on his hip. "I'm gone, Dawn."

"Whyyyy?" Dawn cried, walking out her room pouting. Savage laughed as she walked up to him and he palmed her ass.

"I be back."

"I love you, Savage," Dawn told him.

Savage smacked her ass and walked out of the house.

As soon as Savage hopped in the 650, he knew Freaky had just hit a lick. His wrist was looking too sweet.

"Fuck is up?" Savage greeted, dapping Freaky up as he pulled off.

"Winnin'," Freaky replied laughing. "While you playing house, I'm in a nigga's house tying they ass up, taking they shit," Freaky said, laughing as they cruised up Naylor Road.

"Why you ain't tell me you crushed Smoke's wild ass?" Savage asked, reading a text from Bubbles.

"Fuck you talkin' about?" Freaky asked, playing dumb, as he stopped at the light.

"Stop playing these stupid ass games," Savage said with his eyes on the mirrors. "You did some rookie shit and crushed the nigga by your car. This nigga Greg locked up and Dog still out here somewhere."

Freaky laughed. *Damn, I did some sloppy, rookie shit.*

"I had to crush the nigga, he was doing too much purpin'... Dog next. Fuck all that, doe. We bout to meet up with this nigga about a half a ticket move. He want half doe," Freaky said, making a left on 12th Street.

"Half?" Savage looked at Freaky. "Half of our cut," Savage said as they turned on 10th Place.

"You know we be backdooring shit. I just need to know the move.

He getting backdoored stop, playin' so much," Freaky said as they parked behind an all-white 2019 Audi A6.

Savage looked towards the building and saw people looking their way. His hand went to his F&N, finger on the trigger.

"Didn't Sky's lil ass used to be around here?" Savage asked as he and Freaky hopped out of the 650.

"Yeah, Slim in on a joint."

"Kill," Savage said, following Freaky to the building where the niggas were standing.

Savage's hand was by his waist.

"Freaky." Gucci stepped out the crowd, met Freaky and Savage halfway up the block, and dapped them up.

"You Savage, right?"

"Yeah," Savage said with his hand still by his hip not liking Gucci's energy. He felt that he was a snake.

"Come fuck with me," Gucci told them and stepped off towards the building. They nodded to a few niggas as they followed him in the building.

As soon as they stepped in Apt. 2, they smelled coke in the air. They walked by niggas in the living room bagging up, then walked by the kitchen and saw niggas cooking up. They followed Gucci to the back of the apartment in a room with just a bed and chair in it. Gucci walked to the dresser and leaned on it. Savage still had his hand by his waist. In his eyes, no one present was trustworthy. He glanced at Freaky giving him that look. *We should just brace the whole house.*

Gucci had caught a body back in '07 and got sentenced to 35 years. Everybody turned their backs on him, thinking he was washed up. He stayed in the law library, and after 10 years gave his time back. Everybody that turned their backs, carried him, or played games, he crushed their asses and hit the ground running. He ran it up and took over 10th Place. Gucci was a snake and loyal to nothing... but money.

"Look, Slim," Gucci said, looking at Freaky. "The nigga I was telling you about is named Blaze. The nigga worth a half of ticket, flat-out. I need my cut when you get him." Gucci looked from Freaky to Savage.

Savage was just listening, his body telling him to brace the whole house.

"Blaze is one of them niggas that's gon' die before he give up the money," Gucci said laughing. "But he got a 14-year-old daughter and a wife he'll die for. His daughter go to Brown Jr. High School, his wife drives a 2-door Benz coupe, sky blue joint. She picks her daughter up from school every day... he'll pay for them," Gucci said, pulling his phone out of his pocket. "Here go a picture." Gucci handed Freaky his phone.

Freaky looked at the picture and told him to send the pictures to his phone and handed it back.

"Aye, Gucci, what's up with Sky?" Savage asked.

Gucci laughed. "That's my young nigga. He over the jail fightin' a joint. Hot ass nigga named Duke from up Trinidad tellin' on him."

"Why y'all ain't crush the nigga yet?" Savage asked, looking at Gucci confused.

"Can't get up on the nigga. He be up Trinidad," Gucci said and left it alone.

"Give Sky my number when he call." Savage gave Gucci his number, then they dapped him up and left the apartment.

———

Gucci and his right-hand man, Shooter, stood at the window, watching as Freaky and Savage hopped in the 650 and pulled out.

Gucci was buying work from Blaze but was lining him up because Blaze's wife was Gucci's old bitch before he got locked up. As soon as he went in, Blaze started fucking her. Gucci could've been smoked Duke, but Sky crushed a good man so they said fuck Sky.

"Get Blaze robbed and spanked, then crush Freaky and take everything. Kill two birds with one stone." Gucci laughed and dapped Shooter up.

TWELVE
SAVAGE - 3:40 P.M

"I DON'T LIKE ya man, for real for real. Fuck that nigga! He lucky I ain't rob his wild ass right there," Savage said to Freaky.

Freaky laughed as he pulled off.

"Pull up at Aunt J's house," Savage said. "Finna drop off some money and surprise her."

Savage told Freaky to cut up the music as he thought about crushing the nigga Duke for Sky.

As soon as Freaky pulled in front of Aunt J's house, Savage hopped out smiling to himself as he stepped in Aunt J's building. He opened the front door and heard moaning.

"What the fuck?" he said to himself. Pulling the F&N off his waist, he made his way toward the moaning.

"Ohhhh shit," Aunt J moaned as Dog fucked her from the back. Aunt J had her head in the pillow, ass in the air, high as Dog slid in and out her pussy slow.

"I'm about to nut," Dog said as he pulled his dick out and grabbed Aunt J by the hair. She put his dick in her mouth and started sucking like her life depended on it.

Dog closed his eyes, loving the way Aunt J's mouth felt. Savage was in shock, standing at the door watching his aunt sucking Dog's dick. Savage blacked out, ran to the bed, and smacked Dog with the F&N.

Smack!

Dog's body dropped, and blood spurt on the bed.

"Savage!" Aunt J jumped up in shock, watching as Savage pistol whipped the shit out of Dog. "Stop, Savage stop!" she screamed, watching blood flying all over the bed.

"Fuck you," Savage yelled as he upped the F&N and put it in Dog's face, pulling the trigger.

Boom!

Blood flew on the bed, Savage's face, and all over the dresser.

Aunt J was in shock, screaming at the top of her lungs watching Dog's dead body and the blood pouring out of his head.

"Savage!" Freaky hollered, running in the room. He looked at Aunt J's naked body and Dog laid out with his brains and blood pouring out of his head. Freaky knew Savage had caught Aunt J tricking.

Aunt J had her face in her hands crying, not because of Dog getting killed, but because she saw the hurt on Savage's face.

"Let's go, Moe," Freaky yelled, pulling Savage out of the room.

Savage looked at Aunt J one more time with a disgusted look, then turned and ran out of the house behind Freaky.

"Fuck is you thinkin'. That's some rookie shit," Freaky vented as they hopped in the 650 and pulled off.

"I blacked out, Moe," Savage said, taking off his shirt and wrapping the F&N in it.

"You got blood and shit everywhere, fucking up my seats and shit," Freaky said, pulling on a side street.

Savage hopped out and threw the shirt down a sewage drain.

"You got to lay low for a second. I'ma grab all your shit out the house. Chill till we see what the fucks going on," Freaky said, watching Savage hop back in the 650 with visions of his aunt sucking Dog's dick in his mind.

He was mad as shit as he dialed Cat's number.

———

Cat and V were sitting at the light uptown on their way down Atlanta. Cat grabbed her phone, saw it was Savage calling, looked over at V, winked at him, and sent Savage to voice mail.

"He alright," she said, turning off her phone.

————

"Dumb ass bitch!" Savage yelled. *I ain't talked to this bitch in like two days. Bitch playin' these stupid ass games.* Shaking his head, he dialed Bubble's number as Freaky pulled in the gas station.

Bubbles was walking around her house in a silk robe, sipping a glass of red wine. She looked in the mirror and smiled seeing hickeys all over her neck.

"My baby, Savage. Where the fuck you at lil boy?" She said out loud, grabbing her phone and blushing when she saw he was calling.

"I'm waiting on what's mine, Savage. So you need to pull up," she said with sass in her voice.

"I'm bout to pull up, now."

"I'm waiting, Baby," she told him and hung up.

Savage gave Freaky the address, laid the seat back, and closed his eyes still seeing visions of Aunt J sucking Dog's dick.

THIRTEEN
DETECTIVE GRAM & ROB – 6:02 P.M

"IT'S A FUCKING bloodbath in here. One to the head at close range. This had to be personal," Detective Rob said to his partner as they looked at Dog's dead body. The detective put the sheet back over Dog's face and walked to the living room.

Aunt J was sitting on the couch getting questioned by another detective.

"She says she don't know who the shooter was. He had a mask on. Nobody in the building heard the shot or saw anything... I think it's more to the story. Looks to me like an angry lover caught her fucking a 22-year-old man and couldn't handle it. He blacks out, one shot at close range, snaps out of it, and flees the scene."

"That's what I think," Detective Gram said as he and Detective Rob ducked under the yellow tape and stepped out of the building.

It was a crowd gathered around as they walked to their unmarked cruiser and hopped in.

"We'll just leave the case open. I think we'll find out the true story soon," Detective Rob said to his partner as he pulled off.

BIG MIKE

2 DAYS LATER - 12:50 P.M.

"I saw the news and like the way your peoples handled that situation," the Made Man told Big Mike, sitting a bag of money on the desk as they talked. "This $110,000 for 2 people," he said to Big Mike as he looked him in his eyes.

"That's 180 in 3 days," Big Mike said, looking back into his eyes.

"I'll pay anything for my freedom! My name clean, face good, money ain't shit," the Made Man said seriously.

"I know the police going start watching me more because I've already been questioned about Johnny's murder. I really appreciate you, Slim, straight up. I know you got out the streets but it's only a few real niggas like you left and right now. I need you, Slim. I start trial in 4 months," the Made Man said, shaking his head. "All these so-called real niggas, stand up niggas snitching," he stressed, looking at Big Mike. "Pressure busts pipes. Loyalty's thin, but niggas got me fucked up! If I go to jail, matter fact, fuck jail!" He yelled, slamming his hands on the desk. "I'm cutting my grass, Slim, and killing all snakes and exterminating all rats. Handle this shit for me Slim and I got you." He stood up and shook Big Mike's hand. "It's 5 more of these suckas on the case. The info in the bag is on all of them. I don't want to make your shit hot so next time we meet up at the old spot." The Made Man nodded and left out of the office.

Big Mike took the info out of the bag and shook his head seeing the picture of Curtis Fazon from Simple City.

"Hot ass nigga," Big Mike said to himself looking at the other picture and not knowing the person.

Big Mike took stacks of money out the bag, counting each dollar. He took his $20,000. He knew he could've taken more and Freaky would've still been cool, but that wasn't his swag. He was a straight up real nigga, and he wasn't greedy. He knew what greed led to, a bullet in the head or a jail cell. Plus, Freaky was doing the killing, he just passed off the info. Twenty bands was good enough for him. He put 20 in the safe by the other 20, shut and locked it. Big Mike checked his cameras, grabbed his phone, and called Freaky.

———

"Bitch, why you fakin' like you ain't tryin' to suck my dick?" Freaky said to Tiana as they sat in his 650 parked in front of her building out in Suitland, MD.

"Why you always talking to me like that, Freaky?" Tiana asked, rolling her eyes, looking at the stacks of blue faces sitting in Freaky's lap.

Tiana was a 22-year-old, bad bitch, redbone, body flat out. She had long pretty hair that hung down her back, and Spanish features in her face. Feet a torch, head and pussy a missile. Niggas from all over the DMV area wanted to fuck her. Tiana was IG famous, so she didn't understand why she was still fucking with Freaky and letting him talk to her like she was anything. Tiana didn't know why but Freaky made her pussy soaking wet when she was around him. His swag was on another level. He didn't see anybody, and his pockets were always stuffed and not no skinny shit. He always had bands on him.

"What you gon do, Moe?" Freaky asked, sitting the stack on the dashboard and pulling out his dick.

Tiana rolled her eyes, grabbed his dick, and put her face in his lap.

"Damn! Get that dick sloppy wet for me," Freaky told her as he grabbed his phone off the dashboard. "Yeah," Freaky answered his ringing phone, closing his eyes as Tiana sucked the shit out of his dick.

"We need to talk, ASAP!" Big Mike replied.

Freaky pushed Tiana's head down and grinded in her mouth as he came down her throat.

"I'm bout to pull up in 10 minutes," he said to Big Mike as he rested on the seat to catch his breath as he hung up.

He put the phone on the dashboard as Tiana sucked the tip of his dick, leaned up, and licked his nut off her lips as she looked at him.

Freaky grabbed his bankroll and counted out a band. "Here, Moe, I'm on something."

"Boy, you always fakin'," Tiana said, grabbing the money.

"I'ma call you later. I'm trying to fuck you and Keyshia at the same time... Set it up."

"Whatever," Tiana said, getting out the car.

Freaky put his dick in his pants, grabbed his Glock 22 from under the seat, and sat it on his lap. He beeped the horn at Tiana and pulled off.

Tiana just shook her head as she watched him drive out of the parking lot. She pulled out her phone and called Keyshia so she could do what Freaky asked.

She didn't know why but she was on his dick.

————

Freaky pulled up to Mike's car lot 10 minutes later, parked, and hopped out. He was already hip to what Big Mike was trying to holla at him about. When Freaky stepped in Big Mike's office, Big Mike was sitting behind the desk with a duffle bag in front of him.

"Big Mike, what's up, Slim?" Freaky greeted, taking a seat at the table.

"That's 90 bands for two people. The info's in the bag. We got two days, but..."

"Shit a be done tonight," Freaky said, cutting Big Mike off.

"Get the money. I trust you. I'ma hit yo phone," Big Mike said, looking in Freaky's eyes.

"Bet, watch the news." Freaky grabbed the bag and left out the office.

Mike watched him hop in his 650 and pull off.

"I got you," Big Mike said to himself thinking about the Made Man as he got up and locked up the place. Big Mike was going home to chill with his family.

"You never know when a nigga a put a ticket on your head," he said, laughing and walking to his car.

FOURTEEN
FREAKY – 7:20 P.M

FREAKY PULLED UP AT HOME, walked in, and counted the 90 bands. He took out 25 bands as he read who was on the list. He smiled looking at one picture, putting the other picture and 25 bands in a bag with the info and left out.

As soon as he jumped in the car, he called Savage.

———

"I own you, lil boy." Bubbles laid on Savage, looked him in his eyes, and kissed his face.

Savage palmed her ass, sliding his middle finger in and out of her pussy as she was sucking his bottom lip when his phone rang.

"Hold up, Bubbles."

"No, fuck no Savage. It's my time," she said, trying to hold him down.

Savage flipped her on the bed, got up, and grabbed his phone off the dresser.

"You so fucking pressed. You not going nowhere," she said, getting off the bed in all-black lingerie with her crotch and titties out. She walked to the room door and stood with her arms crossed.

Savage looked at Bubbles shaking his head as he answered the phone.

"You still up Bubbles' joint?" Freaky asked, starting up his car.

"Yeah," Savage said, looking at Bubbles as she stared at him with fire in her eyes.

"I'ma pull up on you, money shit. I'll be there in 20 minutes."

"I'll be ready."

"No he not," Bubbles yelled in the background.

"20, Slim," Freaky said, laughing and hung up.

Savage started getting dressed.

"Savage, I don't know why you getting dressed. You not going no fucking where!" Bubbles roared, walking up and standing in Savage's face.

Savage didn't reply as he put on his shoes. Bubbles grabbed his face. Savage grabbed her by the waist, picked her up, and slammed her on the bed on her stomach and held her down. He pulled his dick out of his pants.

"Get the fuck off me!" Bubbles yelled as Savage slid his dick in her soaking wet pussy. "Stop, get off meee."

"Say I'm sorry," he whispered in her ear, grinding his hard dick in her stomach, hitting all her walls.

"Savage, Ohhhh Savage! "

"Say I'm sorry for fakin'," he said, making her put her ass in the air, face in the pillow.

"Uhnnn, Baby O my Goddd Fuckkk," Bubbles screamed, biting the pillow as Savage pounded her pussy. "I'm sorry, I'm sorry, I love youuu-uu," Bubbles screamed, cumming all over his dick as her body collapsed on the bed, shaking.

Savage got in the pushup position, digging in her pussy.

"Savageeee," Bubbles cried, feeling Savage's nut shooting in her pussy.

Savage pulled out and smacked his dick on her ass. Bubbles laid on her stomach, drained as she watched Savage put on his pants, grab his X-D with the 21 in it, and put it on his hip.

"Be safe, Savage. I got Claw lined up too, Baby," Bubbles said with her eyes getting heavy from the feeling of some good dick. "Can you come back and stay with me tonight, please?" Bubbles asked in a slur.

"I'll be back," Savage vowed, walking out of the room as his phone rang.

"Can you come out and play today?" Freaky asked laughing, pulling up in front of Bubble's building.

"I just crushed her ass, dope dick, you out front?"

"Yeah," Freaky replied and hung up.

"Alright sexy Bubbles!" Savage yelled and walked out of the apartment.

"He fucked the shit out of me," Bubbles said, smiling, and dozed off to sleep.

———

As soon as Savage hopped in the 650, Freaky sat the bag on his lap. Savage opened the bag and saw stacks of blue faces. He looked up at Freaky. Freaky nodded to the papers. Savage looked at one picture and read "Curtis Routine."

Freaky looked at him. "This shit got to be handled today."

"Say no more," Savage said as he dapped Freaky up and hopped out of the 650.

Savage jogged back up to Bubbles' apartment and hid the money in her closet. He took off all his jewelry, sat it on the table, and left out the apartment. He hopped in his Charger, looked at the picture and the info.

"I'ma crush his ass," he said to himself as he pulled off.

FREAKY

7:50 P.M.

Freaky stopped at a surplus store to buy a FedEx outfit, zip ties, and lighter fluid. He hopped in his car, looked at the picture, smiled, and pulled off. He took his time riding up New York Ave., made a right, and pulled up in Ivy City on a side street.

He put on his FedEx outfit and put the zip ties, lighter fluid, and bleach in the FedEx box. He looked at himself in the mirror and pulled off.

Freaky pulled up to West Virginia Ave., parked, and pulled his FedEx mask low over his eyes. He grabbed the box and hopped out of his car. He nodded to a few people as he made his way to building 1722. Walking to Apt. 4, he took the Glock off his hip, and put the hand with the Glock in it under the box. He kicked the door and stepped back when he heard footsteps.

"Who the fuck kicking on my door like they fucking crazy?!" A woman yelled as she snatched open her door.

She stood in some little ass grey workout shorts and a T-shirt with no shoes on her feet looking at Freaky like he was crazy.

"What?!" She yelled.

Freaky grinned and threw the box in her face, rushing her, putting the Glock to her head as he shut the door behind him.

"Don't fucking scream, Dominic," Freaky said, grabbing her by her hair and dragging her in the living room. He pulled down her shorts and made her bend over the edge of the couch.

"Shhhh, do what I say if you want to live," he instructed as he pushed her thong to the side and slid two fingers in and out of her pussy. "We gone have some fun."

SAVAGE

8:15 P.M.

Savage was parked outside of Cutz Barbershop on Alabama Ave. eating a cheeseburger, watching the shop. He watched a lot of people come and go but still didn't see Curtis' Acura pull up yet. He finished the burger and threw the wrapper out of the window.

His heart rate sped up when he saw an all-black Acura pull up and park. He watched Curtis and a dark-skinned lady hop out and walk into the barbershop.

Savage checked the clip on the X-D, cocked it, and made sure everything was right. He put the X-D on his hip, hopped out of the Charger, and walked to the barbershop. He stepped in and took a seat since all of the barber chairs were full. Smiling, he nodded at a young kid and his mother as he watched Curtis kiss the dark-skinned lady on her cheek, get up, and sit in the barber's chair.

Savage got up and walked out of the shop. Hopping in the Charger, he started the car, took his shirt off, and wrapped it around his face. He looked around and saw people minding their business. Taking the X-D off his hip, he took a deep breath and ran to the barbershop.

Curtis' eyes were closed as the barber cut his beard. The barber's eyes grew big at the sight of Savage barreling their way with a gun. He jumped out the way just as Curtis heard screaming, and as he opened his eyes, he saw a flash.

Boom! Boom!

Savage pulled the trigger, hitting Curtis in his cheek and head at close range. He turned and broke out of the barbershop, hopped in his car, and sped off, leaving Curtis's brains on the barbershop's mirror.

Curtis's lady friend was in shock, looking at Curtis fucked over in the barber's chair.

The young nigga that Savage nodded to, left as his mother dragged him out of the shop as soon as Curtis got shot. The young nigga was nervous as he and his mother ran up the block but excited at the same time.

He couldn't wait to tell his friends the gangsta shit he witnessed that day.

FREAKY

"Shittttt," Freaky yelled, nutting all in Dominic's ass before pulling his dick out and slapping it on her asshole. He had her hands cuffed. He fucked her all day, in all of her holes. She didn't want to but the feeling felt too good to her and she came at least 10 times. She was bent over the couch, ass-naked, drained, and couldn't move.

Freaky picked up the Glock and put it to the back of her head. Dominic was in shock and confused, feeling the gun. "Noooo!" she yelled and turned when the first shot went off, hitting her in the back of the neck.

She fell hard on her back, her neck was bleeding bad.

Boom!

Freaky pulled the trigger again and hit her in the head. Her body stopped moving as blood poured out of her wounds like water.

He cleaned up and wiped down everything he touched. He poured bleach and lighter fluid all over the house, then drenched her body and the whole apartment with gasoline. Fixing his clothes, he dropped a match on Dominic's body, and walked out of the apartment. He hopped in his 650, and by the time he pulled off you could see the thick black smoke coming from Dominic's apartment.

FIFTEEN
BIG MIKE

"THIS IS 11:00 P.M. *D.C. News, earlier today, Curtis Fazon, age 29, was gunned down at Cutz Barbershop on Alabama Ave. He's been a government informant since 2010. Curtis was shot twice in the head and face area, the only information that we have received from witnesses was that a man with a shirt over his face ran in the barbershop and killed him.*

On the other side of town, on West Virginia Ave., police responded to a fire and found the body of Dominic Smith, age 35, dead from gunshot wounds to the head and neck. She also had 3rd degree burns all over her body."

"Damn," Big Mike said when his phone rang. He answered and heard, "Good looking," and then a click.

Big Mike smiled and cut off the T.V.

"Good deeds for good men make a nigga feel good," Big Mike said and headed to his son's room to play the game with him thinking, *'life ain't promised to nobody.'*

SKY

D.C. JAIL, THE NEXT DAY – 8:00 A.M

Sky jumped off his bunk and put on his orange and black tag jumpsuit. He washed his face and brushed his teeth. He grabbed his knife from under his pillow, put it in his boxers, and walked out of the cell.

He nodded to a few inmates as he made his way to the phones on the wall. "Lil Mike, what's up?" He greeted a good man, picked up the phone, and dialed Gucci's phone number as he put his back on the wall so he could see the whole unit.

Gucci and Shooter were sitting in his Audi smoking and catching that early morning coke rush when Gucci's phone started ringing.

Gucci handed Shooter the J and answered his phone.

"This Sky bitch ass, " Gucci said to Shooter as he answered his phone.

*"You have a pre-paid call from, **Sky**, press **5** to accept."*

Gucci pressed 5.

"What's up, Moe?" Gucci asked, grabbing the J from Shooter.

"Shit, coolin'. You know I start trial in 4 months, Slim," Sky stressed, watching his cellie walk to the microwave.

"I ain't holla at my uncle yet, it's hard to catch up with the nigga," Gucci said, talking in code about Duke.

Sky just shook his head in frustration.

"Aye, some nigga name Savage gave me his number for you," Gucci let him know, searching through his phone for the number.

"Savage?" Sky was thinking, then he remembered the young nigga that was robbing the whole city.

"You got a pen?" Gucci asked, looking at Savage's number.

"Hold up," Sky said, letting the phone hang. He ran to his cell, grabbed a pen and paper, and jogged back to the phone.

"What is it?" Sky asked.

"2-0-2...5-6-6...9-1-9-1."

"Alright, I'm bout to hit the nigga, get on top of that for me."

"I got you," Gucci lied as he hung up, looking at Shooter. "Fuck that nigga," Gucci said, watching as a junkie walked up.

Sky hung up, and then dialed Savage' s number.

———

"Here Baby," Bubbles said, hopping in her Lex truck and handing Savage his Jordan 12s.

"Let's hit IHOP," he said, sitting the shoes on the backseat when his phone rang. "You drive," Savage told Bubbles, hopping out of the truck and switching seats as he grabbed and answered his phone.

"You have a collect call from -Sky-, Press 5."

Savage pressed 5. "What's up, Slim? Long time," Savage greeted, smiling as Bubbles pulled off.

"Shit, fightin'," Sky said.

"I'm hipped. I'm on top of that shit. Matter fact, pull up Trinidad," Savage told Bubbles. "I don't know what's up with your men. Them niggas wild, throwing me off, straight up," Savage said seriously as Sky laughed.

"I need that ASAP."

"I'm on it, when you start trial?"

"In four months," Sky said, watching the guard making rounds.

"Tier wet!" Sky yelled. "I'm bout to go workout, Slim. I need you," Sky stressed.

"Slim, this Savage!"

"Say no more," Sky said before he hung up and smiled as he walked to the pull up bar.

———

"Pull down 16th, in front of the store," Savage pointed as he put the phone in his pocket.

Bubbles pulled in front of the store and parked. Savage put the Taurus 5th in his pocket.

"Can you hurry up please, baby? I'm hungry," she cried as she leaned over and kissed Savage on his lips.

"Alright," Savage said, hopping out of the truck.

He walked to the store and saw Po sitting on a crate looking at his phone.

Po looked up and Savage, catching him completely off gaurd. "Fuck you doin' on this side of town?" He dapped Savage up.

Po was a hustler, flat out. He wore all foreign clothes and was the type of nigga that a break a whole brick down and sell 50s all month, doing numbers. His face sold.

"Fuck with me," Savage said as they stepped out of the store.

Savage and Po walked up and down the block. Savage put his hand in his hoodie with his finger around the trigger of the 5th.

"What's up with the nigga Duke?" Savage asked, still watching the streets.

"Fuck that hot ass nigga," Po said as a junkie walked up.

Po pulled a sack of rocks out his dip, grabbed a 100 dollar bill from the junkie, and gave her two fat rocks. He put the money in his pocket and the sack back in his dip.

"Why, you want me to throw the oop?" He asked, knowing what type of nigga Savage was.

"No question!" Savage said with his eyes still on the road.

Po went in his pocket and pulled out his phone.

"Give me your number. I'ma hit you as soon as he pull up."

"Bet," Savage said and gave him his number. He dapped Po up and stepped off.

"Hot ass nigga need to die anyway," Po said, walking back in the store.

"I'm hungry, Daddy. You took for fucking ever," Bubbles cried and rolled her eyes at him as she pulled off.

Savage laid his seat back and cut 21 Savage up.

SIXTEEN
V & CAT - 11:50 A.M

V WAS FROM UP DEILFIELD, Uptown. One thing the streets said about V was he was a money getting motherfucker, and he was known to spank something if push came to shove.

V was 28 years old but always heard stories about how good the bitch Cat's head and pussy was. So when he saw her at the mall that day, he couldn't wait to fuck her. That's all he was supposed to do was fuck, but the bitch Cat had him. No bitch ever sucked and fucked him the way she did. And Cat was a fly bitch, hipped to the streets, and she matched his swag. He liked everything about the bitch.

He was falling for her. At first he was taking her to hotels and his little side houses, fucking, but after their trip down Atlanta, he was ready to wife her. He went against everything he stood on and took her to his house. The one he laid his head at out in Upper Marlboro, MD.

He lived in a mini mansion. When Cat stepped in his house she was in awe; she looked around and saw white fluffy carpets that your feet sink into on the floor. Glass tables in the living room, pool table in the middle of the floor, 90-inch flat screen TVs hanging on the wall in every room.

"This nigga got that real money," Cat thought as she took off her heels and let her feet sink into the plush carpet.

V disappeared to his room as Cat looked around and took off her clothes. Her pussy was soaking wet, dripping as she slowly walked to V's room. She looked around and saw V sitting on the bed with a duffle bag in front of him.

V looked up and saw Cat watching him, his dick getting hard just thinking about how her pussy felt.

"Let me count this 200 real quick, Baby," he said and dumped all the money on the floor.

Cat's eyes got big seeing all that money and climbed on the bed to watch V as she ran her finger up and down her clit. She was debating if she should make V hers or should she set the play and get Savage to rob him. Cat smiled at the thought as she slid two fingers in and out her pussy.

FREAKY - 12:10 P.M

"He don't love me no more, Freaky. I fucked up," Aunt J cried as she sat at the table and put a rock in her stem.

She grabbed the lighter, put it to the stem, lit it as she pulled, and exhaled the smoke. She blew out a thick cloud of smoke in the air.

Freaky was watched her nipples got hard, legs opening and closing.

"Savage still love you." Freaky pulled his dick out of his pants, stroking it as he walked up to her. She didn't want to do it but she couldn't help it.

She grabbed Freaky's dick and put it in her mouth. She sucked it as Freaky closed his eyes, loving her mouth. Aunt J had one hand jerking his dick, the other hand rubbing her pussy. She couldn't help it.

BLACK - 1:05 P.M

Black paid for Cash's funeral, dropping 20 bands off to Cash's wife and son. He made a promise before they put Cash in the grave that he was going to kill whoever killed him. After the funeral, it was back to business. Even though he got robbed, the plug still wanted his money. Black paid the plug out of his money, and the money he paid for Cash's funeral, he spent about 75 bands in a week.

Black took his last 40 bands and bought him a brick of powder. Instead of stretching it, he only put enough baking soda on it to lock it up. He was selling all glass, $20 pieces for $50. His pieces were glass, nobody could catch a sell unless he wasn't around. And he wasn't selling weight at all. He was taking the whole brick to the streets, hand-to-hand.

Black was in the trap, bagging up when his phone started ringing. He looked at the caller ID, put the razor down, wiped his hands, grabbed his 357, and ran out the trap.

"Floyd," he called when he saw Floyd in the hallway catching a sell.

As he walked out of the building, he glanced around seeing junkies. He saw a Dodge Neon in the parking lot. He walked to the car and hopped in the passenger seat.

"What's up, Slim?" Tone greeted with his eyes on the mirrors, sliding a bookbag to Black. "That's a brick of dope, give me 100 in 30 days. Tyson gon' slide up on you. I'm bout to lay back for a second," Tone said, never taking his eyes off the mirrors or his surroundings. "You ever found out who did that to Cash?"

"Yeah, bitch named Cat set the play and got some young nigga name Savage to rob us. Shit got ugly. I got a cake baked for him, though."

"Say no more," Tone said and Black hopped out the car.

Tone pulled off thinking of Savage. *I got to do some research on this nigga.*

BUBBLES - 11:40 P.M

Claw picked Bubbles up from the club at 11:40 p.m. He took her out to Brandywine, MD. They were blowing cookie the whole ride. They ate at Checkers, drank a little bit, kicked it, and headed back to the city. Claw eye fucked Bubbles.

She had on an all-black dress that stopped at the top of her thighs, her dreads were pinned up in a bun. She had heels on, showing off her pretty feet. She didn't have on any panties and let him see her pretty pussy all night.

"I want you to fuck me in your car." Bubbles laid her seat back and pulled her dress up to her waist. Putting her feet on the dashboard and spreading her legs, she started playing with her pussy.

Claw knew a cool low-key spot. He touched her pussy and his dick got hard just feeling how wet it was. He was geeking as he drove out to Forestville, MD by the school, parking on a side street.

He was so geeked to fuck, he wasn't watching the mirrors like he usually did. He put the gun on the floor, pulled down his pants, and Bubbles grabbed his dick as he laid back and closed his eyes.

Suddenly, his door was snatched open. He looked up and saw a masked man jamming a big ass gun in his face. Savage pulled him out of the car, pants still by his ankles, cuffed his hands, taped his mouth, and threw him in the trunk of his car. Sprinting back to the driver side, he hopped in, and cranked up the car.

Bubbles got out, fixed her dress, and hopped in the driver's seat of the parked car Savage had been laying in. Seeing the headlights come on and the car come to life, Savage pulled off and Bubbles followed close behind. They hit Claw's spot, and did they thing on him.

Savage came off with 60 bands and gave Bubbles 25. The police found Claw's body two days later in the trunk of a chipped-up Dodge Saturn with multiple wounds to the chest and back area.

Clay Terrace was in an uproar looking for the killer, but nobody knew anything.

Savage and Bubbles didn't have a care in the world and brought in the New Year right. Savage bought an iced out bust down for 20 racks. Bubbles got a new two-door Lex Coupe and let Savage fuck the shit out of her all night.

Happy New Year!

SEVENTEEN
SAVAGE – 2 DAYS LATER

SAVAGE BROUGHT the new year in right. He got dressed, threw on a whole sweat suit with some high-top Givenchy's. He threw on his Savage Shit chain, Big boy flats, and his bust down on his wrist. He had a fresh fade, the high-top blowout. He brought the Glock 18 with the 50 drum on it out. He traded in his Charger and got 15 bands for it, put another 40 with the 15, and got a 2019 SRT Durango, smoke grey, light tints, with the factories still on it.

Savage was looking sweet cruising the streets of DC. Bubbles was blowing up his phone, telling him to come get her or else. Savage just laughed, eyes on the mirrors as he cruised by people at bus stops. They were looking trying to see who the driver was.

"I'll be through later," he told Bubbles as he stopped at the light, clutching the trigger of his 18. *Nobody's taking nothing from me but zombie tips,* Savage thought, keeping his eyes on his surroundings, listening to Bubbles yell and cry telling him she was going to fuck him up.

"Watch!" She said and hung up steaming.

Savage didn't pay her any mind. He was on his way Uptown to fuck with this bad bitch named Nina he met in Saks the day before. He pulled off from the light and made a left on Florida Ave. when his phone rang. He grabbed it, saw it was Po, and answered.

"Slim just pulled up. He leaning on his Escalade truck. He the big strong nigga with them stupid ass glasses on. I'm bout to holla at him, right now."

"Bet. I'm in a smoke grey Durango," Savage said as he hung up.

He made a right up Trinidad, riding up Staples Street. Then a right on Holbrook and another on 16th and Levis. Savage rode by the church and saw Po and Duke talking. Po glanced at the truck and kept talking.

Savage kept driving, then pulled in the alley, and took off his shirt and jewelry. He looked around, but saw no one. Taking a deep breath, he hopped out of the truck with the 18 in his hand. He didn't even wear a mask.

Jogging out of the alley, he ran up to Duke. Po saw him, dapped Duke up, and stepped off. Savage ran up with the 18 in his hand, and Duke felt his presence, prompting him to turn around. ***Boom!***

Savage pulled the trigger, and Duke fell face first on the sidewalk. Savage stood over him and flushed him. People were watching with their mouths wide open as Savage ran off. He hit the alley, hopped in the Durango, and did the dash.

Po watched as people screamed and ran to Duke's body. Po heard the shots. "Fuck that hot ass nigga," he said as he walked in the store and heard the sirens coming.

SKY – D.C JAIL

"Sky, cuff up," the tall, black, muscle bound CO said, standing at Sky's cell with the slot open and handcuffs in his hand.

"For what?" Sky asked, getting off his bunk.

"Legal visit."

"Aight, give me 5 minutes to brush my teeth and shit," Sky said to the CO as he walked to the sink.

"5 minutes," the C.O said as he shut the slot and walked down the tier.

"Fuck is up?" Von asked, looking at Sky from the top bunk.

"I got a legal visit. Hope this shit is good news," Sky said after he finished brushing his teeth.

"No bullshit. You been over this motherfucker for 'bout 3 years," Von said, laughing as he watched Sky put on his fresh jumper.

He put his dreads in a ponytail and threw on his shoes.

"You ready?" The C.O asked.

"Yeah," Sky said as he bent down to get cuffed up.

The C.O cuffed Sky, unlocked and opened the door to let him out, and closed it back behind him.

"When we come off lockdown?" Sky asked as he got escorted off the unit.

"I heard in a week. Y'all got to stop stabbing each other, god damn it," the CO said as he walked to visiting hall number two.

Sky walked inside the visiting hall and sat in front of his lawyer.

"What's up? Good news?" Sky asked.

His lawyer looked up from his paperwork and grinned.

"We're having an emergency hearing tomorrow. Your only witness was gunned down 3 days ago," his lawyer said.

Sky smiled, silently thanking Savage.

"You still got the gun charge pending, but you've been locked up going on 3 ½ years. So I'm going to see if we could get time served," the lawyer said.

Sky just sat there smiling, he couldn't wait to hit the streets.

I owe Savage my life, he thought.

CAT

WOODLAND - 7:40 P.M.

Cat spent the New Year and a couple of more days with V, fucking him crazy. She was really feeling V and still debating on if she was going to get Savage to rob him or not.

"I had so much fun, Baby," Cat said to V as he pulled up in front of her building. She grabbed his face and gave him a big kiss on his lips before grabbing her bags and hopping out of the 550. She blew V a kiss as she walked in her building. When Cat stepped in her building, she saw Black, Floyd, Tim, and Tom blocking the steps.

"Move, fuck!" Cat yelled as she walked pass. "Broke ass niggas!" She yelled as she unlocked her door, stepped in, and locked the door behind her.

Cat had her phone off the whole week. "I miss my Savage. I know he mad I ain't been answering," she said to herself as she walked in her room. "I'ma make it up to him." Putting her bags in the closet, she took off her clothes and sat on the bed as she dialed Savage's number.

————

"Savage, you not that fucking cute Lil Boy, stop fucking playing with me!" Bubbles said as she watched Savage get dressed. He threw on all his jewelry.

Bubbles was really in love with Savage.

"You on my dick," Savage said, leaning on the dresser to twist up some gas.

"Who you talking to like that?" Bubbles got off the bed in just her thong and bra as she walked up to him.

"You," Savage replied, firing up his J.

Bubbles stood in front of him and looked in his eyes. He grabbed her by the ass and pulled her to him, as he blew gas in the air. Bubbles kissed him on his lips and grabbed the J out of his hand.

"You lucky I'm letting you go outside today. I should make you stay in the house and fuck the shit out you. Say something smart," she taunted and hit the J as Savage pushed her thong to the side and ran his finger up and down her slit.

"Sssss," she moaned as she cocked her legs open and blew gas in the air. "So, be happy," she grinded on his fingers and looked in his eyes when his phone rang.

"That better not be no bitch neither." Bubbles sat the J on the dresser, biting and sucking his neck.

"Can I get the phone, please?" Savage asked, shaking his head.

She stepped back and watched as Savage grabbed his phone out his pocket. Bubbles stared right in his face.

"Watch out," Savage told her and turned the other way.

"Savage, I can be in your face," she said, grabbing his face and turning it to her.

Savage looked at the caller ID. "This Cat."

"So fucking what, you mine now," she proclaimed as she watched him answer.

"What's up?"

"Heyyy, Boo," Cat greeted with a smile, missing his voice.

"Boo? Oh, yeah?" Savage laughed. "Your phone been off all week."

"You don't have to explain yourself," Bubbles yelled in the background, rolling her eyes.

"Who is that?" Cat asked, sitting up in her bed wondering who Savage was around.

Bubbles heard Cat and snatched the phone from Savage and stated, "This Bubbles, bitch!"

"Bubbles?" Cat said sarcastically and laughed, but she was steaming on the inside. "Bitch, you ain't nothing but a fuck and good pussy licker. Savage know where home is, you bum ass bitch."

"Bum? Bitch, fuck you!" Bubbles yelled when Savage snatched the phone out of her hands.

Bubbles was steaming mad, pacing, and thinking about going over to Cat's house and beating her ass.

"Hello, so that's how you want to play, Savage? You know what? I'ma burn and throw away all this shit in 20 minutes if you don't get here now bitch!" Cat hollered and hung up. "I'ma fuck his ass up and that snake ass bitch, Bubbles. Ughh! I need some fucking weed," Cat vented as she got out of the bed, threw on some sweats, a t-shirt, and her slippers. She walked to the door and stepped in the hallway.

Black and Tom were sitting on the steps. Floyd and Tim were leaning on the side of her door.

"Black, give me some fucking weed," Cat said, looking at him.

Tim looked at Floyd, then slid behind Cat and put her in a choke-hold, cutting off her windpipe. He drug her into her apartment.

Black looked around for witnesses, then nodded to Tom and walked in shutting the door behind them.

CHAPTERS 18

"Bitch, you got me fucked up, running to that bitch. You ain't going no fucking where," Bubbles yelled, blocking the room door.

"Watch out, Moe," Savage said, walking towards her.

"Bitchhh!" Bubbles screamed and swung on him. Savage ducked, pushed her out of the way, and ran out the apartment.

Bubbles chased him all the way to the hallway door, still in her thong and bra.

"Bitch, I'ma fuck you up!" Bubbles screamed, running back in the house. She put on some pants, shoes, and a shirt. Grabbing her keys and mace, she ran out of the house. "Savage got me fucked up!"

———

"You thought a nigga wasn't hip to you?" Black asked, smacking the shit out of Cat.

Cat grabbed her face as tears rolled down her face.

"Call Savage. Get him over here now!" Black ordered, putting his 44 in her face. He handed her the phone, she grabbed it and dialed Savage's number.

I don't want to die, she thought.

———

Savage was doing the dash, running lights, flying to Cat's house when his phone started to ring. He saw it was Cat and answered.

"5 minutes," Cat said and hung up.

Black pulled a gun from his waistline, and drew down on Cat. "What the fuck was that? Some sort of distress call or something!?"

"No! Black! I swear!"

"Well, speak bitch!" Spit flew from Blacks mouth, his brows creased in anger. "Cause from where I stand that's exactly what it sounded like!"

Cat put her hands out in front of her. "No! I, I just got off the phone with him before y'all came. I been out of state and haven't been answering my phone so he's tripping on me with another bitch. I told him he had twenty minutes to get here or I'm burning all his shit."

Black let his arm fall to his side. He looked from Floyd to Tim and Tom, and trained his gun back on Cat.

"Please," Cat cried. "Don't Black, I'm..."

Black pulled the trigger.

Boom!

The bullet struck Cat in the chest, sending her back to the floor in a heap. Dark, crimson blood poured from her sternum and leaked from the side of her mouth as she gasped for air, eyes wide with fear. This was the end and she knew it.

Black turned around. "Search this motherfucka!"

————

Savage pulled up to Cat's house, hopped out the car, and jogged straight up to Cat's apartment. He was so focused on his money and guns that he wasn't paying attention to his surroundings. "Aye, Cat, don't touch my shit!" Savage yelled, hearing movement in Cat's room. "Cat don't fuck with my shit!" He yelled and opened the door. He saw blood everywhere and froze as a gun got jammed into his face. He saw a flash.

Boom!

Savage's body hit the floor.

"That's for Cash, you bitch ass nigga!" Floyd said before he snatched Savage's chain.

Blood got in Savage's eyes as everything went black.

————

Bubbles pulled up and stopped her car right beside Savage's car. She hopped out and saw four dudes running out the building. Bubbles ran in the building, mace in her hand, as she ran in Cat's house.

"Savage?" She called and froze. She almost threw up seeing Cat's dead body on the floor, with blood pouring out her head.

"Noooo!" She screamed when she saw Savage. She grabbed her phone and ran over to him. She held him as he bled out on the floor.

"We need help! We need help!" Bubbles screamed into the phone, crying as she rocked Savage. "Don't die Baby, please... don't die!" She held him with blood leaking everywhere as she waited for help.

EIGHTEEN

"BITCH, you got me fucked up, running to that bitch. You ain't going no fucking where," Bubbles yelled, blocking the room door.

"Watch out, Moe," Savage said, walking towards her.

"Bitchhh!" Bubbles screamed and swung on him. Savage ducked, pushed her out of the way, and ran out the apartment.

Bubbles chased him all the way to the hallway door, still in her thong and bra.

"Bitch, I'ma fuck you up!" Bubbles screamed, running back in the house. She put on some pants, shoes, and a shirt. Grabbing her keys and mace, she ran out of the house. "Savage got me fucked up!"

———

"You thought a nigga wasn't hip to you?" Black asked, smacking the shit out of Cat.

Cat grabbed her face as tears rolled down her face.

"Call Savage. Get him over here now!" Black ordered, putting his 44 in her face. He handed her the phone, she grabbed it and dialed Savage's number.

I don't want to die, she thought.

———

Savage was doing the dash, running lights, flying to Cat's house when his phone started to ring. He saw it was Cat and answered.

"5 minutes," Cat said and hung up.

Black pulled a gun from his waistline, and drew down on Cat. "What the fuck was that? Some sort of distress call or something!?"

"No! Black! I swear!"

"Well, speak bitch!" Spit flew from Blacks mouth, his brows creased in anger. "Cause from where I stand that's exactly what it sounded like!"

Cat put her hands out in front of her. "No! I, I just got off the phone with him before y'all came. I been out of state and haven't been answering my phone so he's tripping on me with another bitch. I told him he had twenty minutes to get here or I'm burning all his shit."

Black let his arm fall to his side. He looked from Floyd to Tim and Tom, and trained his gun back on Cat.

"Please," Cat cried. "Don't Black, I'm..."

Black pulled the trigger.

Boom!

The bullet struck Cat in the chest, sending her back to the floor in a heap. Dark, crimson blood poured from her sternum and leaked from the side of her mouth as she gasped for air, eyes wide with fear. This was the end and she knew it.

Black turned around. "Search this motherfucka!"

———

Savage pulled up to Cat's house, hopped out the car, and jogged straight up to Cat's apartment. He was so focused on his money and guns that he wasn't paying attention to his surroundings. "Aye, Cat, don't touch my shit!" Savage yelled, hearing movement in Cat's room. "Cat don't fuck with my shit!" He yelled and opened the door. He saw blood everywhere and froze as a gun got jammed into his face. He saw a flash.

Boom!

Savage's body hit the floor.

"That's for Cash, you bitch ass nigga!" Floyd said before he snatched Savage's chain.

Blood got in Savage's eyes as everything went black.

———

Bubbles pulled up and stopped her car right beside Savage's car. She hopped out and saw four dudes running out the building. Bubbles ran in the building, mace in her hand, as she ran in Cat's house.

"Savage?" She called and froze. She almost threw up seeing Cat's dead body on the floor, with blood pouring out her head.

"Noooo!" She screamed when she saw Savage. She grabbed her phone and ran over to him. She held him as he bled out on the floor.

"We need help! We need help!" Bubbles screamed into the phone, crying as she rocked Savage. "Don't die Baby, please... don't die!" She held him with blood leaking everywhere as she waited for help.

NINETEEN

HUNTWOOD APARTMENTS – 12:30 P.M

PAM TOLD her father she was spending the night over Jaz' house and Jaz told her mother she was spending the night over Pam's house. They both lied and ended up at Freaky's house.

"Shhhhh," Freaky whispered in Jaz' ear as she was laying on her stomach, on the floor in just her bra. Freaky was behind her in push-up position, sliding his dick in and out of her pussy.

"Ohhh," Jaz moaned, biting her lip as Freaky got deeper.

Pam was on the couch faking like she was sleep. She was watching on the low and couldn't wait until he fucked her. Freaky sped up, feeling his nut building when his phone rang.

"Uhnnn, ohhh, Freakyyy!" Jaz screamed as he pounded faster and harder.

Freaky pulled out and nutted all over her ass cheeks. His dick was coated white with her cream. He stood up and grabbed his phone.

"Yeah," he answered and heard screaming.

"Savage got shot in his head. He's in a coma at Providence Hospital right now in Room 301," Aunt J yelled like she was having a break-down as she looked at Savage, praying he made it.

"What?!" Freaky ran in his room, threw some clothes on, grabbed the Kemba 5th, with the 25 in it, and ran out of the apartment.

Pam leaned up on the couch looking at Jaz. Jaz was in the same position, feeling good, coming down off her cloud of satisfaction.

"Girl, don't think cause he fucked you first, he want you. That's *my* dude!" Pam said, looking at Jaz and rolling her eyes.

———

Freaky pulled up at Providence, put the Kemba on his hip, hopped out of the 650, and ran in the hospital. He jogged to room 301, walked in and froze when he saw Aunt J and Bubbles sitting by Savage's bed crying.

He looked at Savage. "Damn, Slim."His heart was heavy seeing his young nigga laying there in a coma with tubes and needles sticking out of his body. "Fuck happened?" Freaky asked, shaking his head with murder on his mind as he looked at Bubbles for answers.

"I saw four dudes running out of Cat's building," Bubbles said still in her bloody clothes, stressed with tears rolling down her face. "I ran in the house and saw Cat dead and Savage," she got choked up. "I thought he was dead, too," Bubbles said and busted out crying.

"Alright," Freaky said, turning to walk out the door when Detectives Rob and Gram stepped in.

Detective Rob looked at Freaky but Freaky didn't look at them as he walked out of the room. He had the 5th on him.

"Sir!" Detective Rob tried to call him but Freaky was gone. Detective Rob looked from Savage, to a bloody Bubbles, to Aunt J.

Didn't a guy just get killed in her house a week ago, he thought. "Ma'am—"

"Before you even ask, I don't know nothing," Aunt J said, cutting him off before he could start.

Bubbles looked at Detective Gram. "Me either!"

The detectives looked at each other. They weren't about to get anything from the women; not tonight.

"If y'all remember anything, give us a call," Detective Gram handed both of them his card.

The two detectives looked at Savage again and walked out of the room.

"What you think?" Detective Gram asked as they walked down the hall.

"I think I remember the guy that just walked out of the room. I think his name is Damian, they call him Freaky. I remember him from my days working the beat on the Southside. The guy that's in the coma, his name is Trey Johnson, but they call him Young Savage. His father was Big Savage, I saw the pictures in the house the day when the guy got killed there." Detective Rob said as they walked out of the hospital to their unmarked car. "They say Lil Savage is just like his father, and I know Freaky from back in the day. He's a killer and a fucking pervert, rapist motherfucker. Let's pull up Woodland. I got a feeling shit is about to get real fucking ugly in the city. Plus, I think I got an idea who that lady in there was protecting." Detective Rob said as he pulled off.

———

Freaky gripped the 5th on his lap, finger on the trigger as he rode up Woodland. *I'm bout to flush one of these niggas.*

When he pulled in Cat's complex, he saw Tim, Tom, Floyd, Black, and a couple of niggas watching him with their hands on their hips, clutching and mugging.

Floyd and Freaky caught eye contact, but Freaky kept driving as he pulled out his phone and called Nook. He needed answers.

Detectives Rob and Gram were riding in the complex. They caught eye contact with Freaky, but he turned his head and kept driving.

"Yeah, shit's about to get ugly," Detective Rob said to Gram as they parked in front of Cat's building.

Nook answered on the first ring, as Freaky pulled in Giant's parking lot and parked.

"Niggas shot my Lil Man up Woodland. I need answers, now!"

"I'm on it," Nook said and hung up.

Freaky was frustrated, angry, and shaking as he twisted up, waiting on Nook's call. His trigger finger was itching. He wanted to kill something. Taking two deep pulls from the J, he blew the smoke out his nose trying to calm his nerves when his phone rung. He grabbed it and answered on the first ring.

"Look, my cousin D-Boy be up the lane. He say the bitch Cat set a play for Savage to brace Black and Cash. Cash bucked and got fucked around." Nook looked out of the window, watching his sister walk in the building across the street with two niggas. *Thot ass.*

"D-Boy say Floyd peeped the play. They caught Savage and Cat lacking and shit got ugly," Nook said as he walked to his room.

Freaky was shaking his head. *I told the nigga to leave that bitch Cat alone.*

"D-Boy said give him 10 bands, he'll throw the oop ASAP."

"Bet! Tell 'em I said set up ASAP! Bout to go grab the money, now." Freaky hung up the phone and pulled off. *Everybody that had a hand in that shit is getting crushed, too.*

TWENTY
DETECTIVE ROB AND GRAM – 5:30 P.M

"I DON'T KNOW the full story with the kid Savage. I only heard bits and pieces about him killing Cash, but I know that's the reason he's in a coma and his lady friend got killed. Savage has a friend named Damian Jones. They call him Freaky. I've ran into him twice today. He has a history of violence and putting his dick in anything that has a hole. He's been like this since a kid, so I need everyone riding around asking questions. I need info on where Freaky lays his head and a 24/7 a day watch on Savage just in case he comes out of his coma. I want the full story A-S-A-fucking-P, so keep your ears and eyes to the streets. Meeting's over." Detective Rob dismissed his team as he grabbed his coat and looked at his partner. "I don't know why, but I got a feeling someone's going to die today."

BLACK AND FLOYD
WOODLAND - 11:50 P.M

"We partying for Cash tonight," Black yelled as him, Tim, Tom, Floyd, & D-Boy sat in front of the trap.

Floyd was fly as shit, Versace down from his shades to his feet. He had Savage's "Savage Shit" chain around his neck, Savage's Glock 22 on his hip and 15 bands of Savage's money in his pocket.

They came up on 63 bands and 7 guns. They split the money four ways, getting 15 a piece, three bands went to more guns. Everybody was fly, and Black was smiling ear-to-ear.

"We partying for Cash!" Black yelled. "We sliding up Exotics and doing us."

"No question," Tim replied geeking.

"Let's hit 51/51 Liquor store first. Get that White Remy. You know they only sell champagne at Exotics." D-Boy said to Floyd grinning.

"Naw, fuck that! We drinking Ace for my man!" Black said as they walked to his truck.

"Floyd, come on, Slim. You already know that White is our mix. We'll meet him at the club," D-Boy stressed, looking at Floyd with that, *we need that* look.

"You right, Slim. I need that White in my system," Floyd said, feeling himself.

Black looked at him confused, "Moe, we bout to leave now, Slim."

"Me & D-Boy gon' meet y'all there."

"Alright, Slim," Black said, not really wanting him to go with Freaky still out and about. Floyd saw what he was thinking and lifted up his shirt, showing the Glock on him. "I'm cool, Slim."

"Alright," Black said dapping Floyd up.

D-Boy walked off to the rear and pulled out his phone to call Freaky.

———

"Bet back broke nigga, this shit too long," Freaky yelled, picking another knot up off the hallway floor. Freaky and Nook were in Nook's building up in Simple City shooting dice with Killa and L.

Killa and L were right-hand men. You never saw one without the other. They robbed and jacked cars. They were plugged in with a chop shop getting six bands a car so you knew they're always lurking and they had a team that was on all work call shit.

Killa was mad as shit. He came in the game with five bands. He was down to his last $500.

"Bet nigga," Killa said to him and dropped his last $500 on the floor.

Nook and L were just sitting on the steps smoking and watching.

Freaky grabbed the dice when his phone rang. "Hold up," he told Killa, as he grabbed his phone and answered.

"51/51 Liquor store now!" D-Boy said and hung up as he hopped in the car.

"I'm gone," Freaky said, walking out of the building when Killa grabbed his arm.

"Fuck you mean, let me win my money back."

"What?" Freaky snatched his arm away. "I'm gone," Freaky said and jogged out of the building with murder on his mind.

Killa picked his money up and looked at L, L knew that look.

"Bitch ass nigga got me fucked up," Killa said and left out of the building.

Nook didn't say anything, he just shook his head.

———

"We bout to look sweet," Floyd bragged as he and D-Boy pulled up to 51/51 Liquor, parked, and hopped out. They walked in the store and Floyd walked up to the counter and pulled out a big ass bankroll.

"Let me get a 5th of that White Remy and some sheets," he said to the clerk, flipping through his money.

Freaky pulled up to the liquor store, put his hood on his head, grabbed his Kemba, and hopped out. D-Boy saw Freaky walk into the store and backed up.

Floyd was grabbing his bottle and turned.

Boom!

Freaky shot him in his face. Floyd fell face first, the liquor bottle fell and busted all over the floor. People were screaming, scared, and running out of the store. Freaky stood over Floyd and put the whole 25 in him. Floyd's body jerked and twitched with each shot.

Freaky snatched the chain off Floyd's neck and broke out of the store.

"Bitch ass nigga," he said to himself as he hopped in the car and did the dash.

D-Boy was stuck in shock, he never saw anybody work like that. Blood was everywhere. D-Boy threw up looking at Floyd's dead body.

BLACK – 1:40 A.M

Black, Tim, Tom, and Greg were in the club purping, buying out the bar. All you saw was bottles of Ace with the sparkles going to their V.I.P. section. They were all booted up off that Molly, throwing money, looking sweet. Plus, they had all the baddest strippers in their section sucking dick and doing it all. They were lit and forgot all about Floyd and D-Boy.

"R.I.P. Cash," they all yelled standing on couches, making it rain.

If only they knew their man was getting rolled out on a gurney as they partied.

TWENTY-ONE
FREAKY - 1:59 A.M

AFTER FREAKY KILLED FLOYD, he got rid of the dog, changed his clothes, and stopped home to grab another 5th. He hit the South-side, got some perk 30s, and three lines of lean and slid back to Nook's house. Freaky was smoking gas, watching Nook sipping his second line of Red and his third perk 30. He watched Nook going in and out of a nod. When Nook started snoring, Freaky stood up, called his name, and shook him. Nook was out of it.

Freaky walked down the hallway and opened his little sister's door. She was laying on her side with her back facing the door. She had on a little white T-shirt and a thong. She knew Freaky was in the living room and knew how her brother got, always passing out off the perks. She was playing with herself, hoping Freaky came to her room. She stopped and acted like she was sleep when she heard footsteps walking down the hallway.

"Jammy," Freaky whispered as he shut her door and walked up to her bed. He laid the 5th on the floor, pulled his dick out of his sweats, and climbed in the bed behind her.

Jammy was still faking like she was sleep as she felt Freaky sliding her thong down her thighs. She bit her bottom lip feeling Freaky's dick sliding in her pussy.

"Ssssss," she let out a moan as Freaky held her shoulders sliding in and out of her pussy slow.

"Damn, this pussy good," Freaky whispered in her ear as he rolled her on her stomach. She still had her eyes closed, arching her back, letting him slide in her deeper. "You like this dick?" Freaky asked, speeding up his stroke.

"Yessss, ohh yesssss," Jammy moaned as Freaky made her get on her knees. She arched her back, putting her face down in the pillow, ass up. Freaky grabbed her waist and punished her pussy. "Uhnnn, shit ohhhh… it's too deeeep. Freaky, I'm cummminnggg," Jammy cried, biting the pillow.

Clap! Clap! Clap!

The sound of her ass meeting his pelvis was all to be heard.

"Cum on this dick, cum on it," Freaky said, trying to put his dick in her stomach.

"I'm cummming," Jammy screamed, cumming as her body went limp.

"Fuckkk," Freaky whispered, cumming all in Jammy's pussy, collapsing on her back.

Jammy was smiling to herself, loving how his dick felt in her walls.

Freaky slid his dick out of her and smacked it all over her ass cheeks.

"Jammy," he called, she looked up at him as he put his dick in her face. She grabbed it and started sucking it while looking in his eyes. All you heard was slurping and Nook snoring as Freaky fucked his man's little sister.

DETECTIVE ROB & GRAM

51/51 LIQUOR STORE – 2:01 A.M

Detective Rob lifted the sheet and looked at Floyd's dead body. "I knew it! It was fucking overkill. Witnesses say it was someone with a hood on their head. That' s all they saw, too."

"D-Boy's in shock. He acts like he doesn't remember anything."

"Hey, Gram," a skinny, white female officer with blonde hair called, walking up to him with a security tape in her hand.

"Hopefully, we can find the killer. Although I must say I have a strong idea who it is," Detective Rob said as they walked out the liquor store. He looked at Gram. "I bet my life it was Freaky." He hopped in the car, smacking the tape on his thigh.

BLACK

NEW YORK AVE. - 7:40A.M

Black woke up at 7:39a.m. ass naked, mouth dry, and head aching. He looked around the hotel room and saw two naked strippers lying beside him. Black got up, flushed the condom he still had on, took a piss, and got dressed. He put a couple of hunnids on the table and was headed out of the room when the T.V. caught his attention He stopped when he saw 51/51 Liquor store taped off. "Fuck happened there?" Black said to himself, walking to the T.V. and cutting it up.

"This is D.C. News. Last night marks the 20th murder of this year and it's only January 12, 2020. Last night, Floyd Johnson age 19…"

"What the fuck?" Black yelled as his heart dropped in his stomach. He saw his little man's face flash across the T.V. screen, and cut the T.V. up.

"Floyd Johnson was killed in this liquor store behind me," the reporter said as the cameraman put the camera on the store. *"This was one of the most gruesome murders this year. Floyd was shot over 20 times in his…"*

"Fucckkkk!" Black yelled with tears rolling down his face. He stormed out of the hotel room and pulled out his phone. Someone was going to answer for this.

TWENTY-TWO
FREAKY

SIMPLE CITY - 7:50 A.M

"OHHHHH, UHNNN, FREAKKKYYY. OH MY GODDD," Jammy cried, biting Freaky's chest, cumming again and almost passing out.

Freaky was digging his dick deep in Jammy, cumming inside her. He pulled his dick out and smacked it against her clit. Freaky fucked Jammy all night, sucking her pussy and ass. He touched every part of her body. Jammy had never been fucked like that and was in pure bliss.

As she watched Freaky pulling up his pants, she couldn't move. Her legs were cocked open, pussy coated white as nut rolled down her thighs. Freaky put the 5th in his hoodie, gave Jammy a kiss on the lips, and put the cover over her. She grinned, eyes heavy as she dozed off. She was in heaven as Freaky walked out of her room.

Nook was still on the couch snoring. Freaky went in Nook's pocket and took his bankroll. "You don't need that," he said as he walked out of the apartment. He put his hand in his hoodie, gripping his strap, finger on the trigger as he walked down the steps. He was to the hallway door when Killa walked in the building.

"What's up with that purping shit last night?" Killa asked, looking in Freaky's face.

Freaky looked at Killa like he was stupid and Killa busted off on him.

"Fuck!" Freaky fell against the hallway's wall.

Killa grabbed his shirt, and Freaky whipped out the 5th, pointed it center mass and pulled the trigger.

Boom!

Killa's eyes got wide as he grabbed his chest.

Freaky pushed him to the floor, and stood over him.

Boom! Boom!

He put the 5th back in his hoodie and threw on his hood as Killa laid on the hallway floor leaking out. Freaky stepped out into the morning sun, speed walking to his 650. A couple people heard the shots and were watching Freaky as they made their way to Nook's building.

Freaky didn't look back as he hopped in the 650 and pulled off. When he got to the bottom of the hill, he looked in the mirror and saw his eye swelling up. He pulled off riding up Benning Road.

"I'm still the sexiest nigga in the city. Stupid nigga!" He laughed and thought about Killa as he cut up the radio and headed home. He was tired as shit.

DETECTIVES ROB & GRAM

POLICE STATION - 11:50 A.M.

"What you think?" Detective Rob asked his partner as he rewound the video for the 100th time. They were in a small white office room inside the precinct reviewing the surveillance footage from the liquor store.

"I'm not going to lie, I can't see his face." Detective Gram took a closer look at the video.

"But it's Freaky, right?" Detective Rob asked but he already knew the answer.

"As bad as I want it to be, I can't see his face." Detective Gram watched the hooded figure snatch a chain off Floyd's neck. "Hold on. Freeze frame that."

"What?"

"Go back."

"Back?"

"Yea," Detective Gram said. "Go back to when he snatches the chain of his neck."

Detective Rob tapped a key on the desktop, taking it back a few seconds.

"There!" Detective Gram pointed at the screen. "Now, zoom in. What's that say?"

"Savage Shit. I bet that's Savage's chain." Detective Rob looked back at his partner. "Still don't believe Freaky killed Floyd?"

Detective Gram stared at the screen.

BLACK
WOODLAND - 12:02 P.M

Black pulled up to Woodland and grabbed his .357 off his lap. He hopped out of his truck and walked in the building. He stepped in the trap and saw D-Boy and Tim talking. He walked right up to D-Boy, pushed him to the wall, and put the .357 to his lips and asked,

"What the fuck happened to my Lil Man?!" He yelled, staring in D-Boy's eyes.

This nigga hip to me? D-Boy was scared, shaking. "Slim, shit happened too fast. The nigga Freaky caught us lacking," D-Boy told, throwing Freaky under the bus. He didn't give a damn! At that point, all he cared about was saving himself.

Black stared daggers through D-Boy. Everything in him telling him to put his brains on the wall. He looked in his eyes, took a deep breath, and walked away.

D-Boy closed his eyes, his heart pumping rapidly in his chest. He looked at Black as he paced the room. *I'ma throw the oop on yo bitch ass next.*

TWENTY-THREE
BIG MIKE

4 days later, Jonesville, VA - 6:20 p.m.

"WHAT'S UP, SLIM?" The Made Man greeted, dapping Big Mike up as they sat at a bar called *Jones* in deep Jonesville, VA. This spot was where they copped their first fifty bricks from the plug back in the 90s.

"Same shit, Slim. Happy to still be above ground and out of one of them cells," Mike told him, taking a sip of his drink.

"No question. Shit starting to get tight, Slim. My lawyer said three witnesses got killed. They saying it's me but ain't got no proof. Four more motherfuckers and I'm home free, Slim. I got 280k in the car and the info on all of them and their whereabouts. Four months Slim."

"I got you." Big Mike stood, dapped the Made Man up and walked out the bar.

The Made Man watched Big Mike as he made his *exit. We need more real niggas like him.*

FREAKY - 12:50 A.M

"She wit whatever I'm wit'. We ballin' together, it's never gon' stop."

Moneybagg Yo blasted out of the speakers. Freaky sat in the Jacuzzi in his $1000 a night hotel suite, blowing sheets of gas, sipping Rosé with all his jewelry on. He eyed Tiana and her best friend, Keyshia walking around the room naked.

He stood up naked, dick swinging as he climbed out of the Jacuzzi. Tiana and Keyshia sat on the bed, watching him.

I love this nigga, Tiana thought.

Keyshia been on Freaky's dick. She had never run into anybody like him and was willing to do anything for him. Freaky walked right up to Keyshia and put his dick in her face. He grabbed Tiana's hand, stood her up, and kissed her as Keyshia sucked his dick. Tiana sucked his lip and let it go. Freaky hit the J as Tiana pulled his dick out of Keyshia's mouth, put it in hers, and went to work.

Keyshia laid back on the bed, put her legs in the air, fingered her phat pussy, watching Freaky as he smoked gas and sipped Rosé enjoying his night.

BIG MIKE'S CAR LOT - 11:40 P.M

Big Mike made it back to the city safe and sound, with 280 thousand dollars and the info on four people that had a couple more days to live.

Big Mike walked in his office, sat at the table, and counted each dollar, taking eighty for himself.

"After this, I'm out," he said to himself as he watched the cameras. He looked at the pictures and the info and couldn't believe these four were telling. "So called stand up men!" He shook his head. *That's why I'm out of the game. This shit is too watered down.*

He was always taught to have an out-plan and never let greed take over. You had to have goals and when it was done... walk away. He was done.

Mike pulled out his phone to call Freaky.

————

Freaky was on his eighth J, had downed two bottles of Rosé, and had fucked Tiana and Keyshia in their asses, pussies, and mouths. Freaky was high as shit, sitting back in the chair, smoking, and watching Keyshia and Tiana eating each other out.

"My young nigga Savage need to wake the fuck up and enjoy this shit," he slurred feeling good off that good cookie and Rosé. His phone rang at the same time Keyshia climbed off the bed and walked towards him.

Keyshia was brown-skinned, with big thighs, and a phat ass, but little titties. Her face was cute, with shoulder length hair. But her biggest asset was her phat pretty ass pussy, she had a big phat pussy and a phat clit that you could see poking through her pussy lips. She walked right up to Freaky and grabbed his dick. Turning around with her ass facing him, she rubbed his dick all over her pussy, and slid it in her, sliding all the way down on it.

Freaky sat the J in the ashtray. He'd heard his phone but ignored it, watching Keyshia sliding up and down on his dick faster.

Keyshia arched her back and put her hands on the floor, "Freakyyy," she moaned, grinding hard on his dick. "I love it, shiittt, this dick feel so good!" She screamed while still grinding her pussy in a circle as his dick hit all her walls. Freaky's dick hit her G-spot and Tiana watched from the bed.

"Freaky. I'ma cum right nowwww!" Keyshia yelled. Jumping off his dick, she rubbed her clit fast, squirting all over the chair. She fell on her back, breathing hard, drained.

Freaky looked at Tiana, his dick still hard. Tiana grinned, climbed out of the bed, walked up to him and put his dick in her mouth. His phone rang again and this time, he grabbed it off the table, and looked at the Caller I.D. Grabbing a handful of Tiana's hair, he started fucking her mouth as the phone rang. Tiana continued to suck as he fucked her face.

"Shittt!" Freaky yelled as he shot a big load of nut in her mouth. He laid back in the chair, and watched Tiana swallow his nut. Catching his breath, he answered the phone, slurring. "Yeah."

"I got business to talk about. Pull up on me," Big Mike said, glancing at his watch, knowing his wife was probably mad as hell.

"Alright, give me 30 minutes. I'm out in VA."

"Time is money, soldier. I'ma hold you to 30 minutes, but if you ain't here in an hour, I'ma catch you tomorrow."

"I'm on my way," Freaky said and hung up.

Money was the thing on his mind. Freaky got up and got dressed, putting his gun on his hip.

"Where you going?" Tiana asked watching Freaky pull out his bankroll and count out three bands.

"This 3 bands for y'all. I'm on something," he said as he put the money on the table. "If I'm not back, catch an Uber. I'ma holla at y'all," he told them and jogged out of the hotel room.

"He think he all that," Tiana commented, smiling as she counted out $1500 and handed Keyshia her half.

"He is, bitch, don't fake," Keyshia said, laughing and counting her money.

————

Freaky pulled up to Mike's car lot 40 minutes later. It was 1:20a.m. when he parked and hopped out of his 650.

Mike met him at the office door with the duffle bag in his hands. "That's 200. The info is in the bag, too. I need that shit done before the months out, if at all possible," he said to Freaky as he handed him the bag and locked up his office.

"I'm on it," Freaky assured him.

"What's up with Savage?" Big Mike asked as they walked to their cars.

"Slim in a coma. He got hit in the head. He gon' make it, doe. He just gettin' his rest in. I got you on this doe," Freaky told Big Mike before he hopped in his car and pulled off.

"Damn." Big Mike said a quick prayer for Savage. "Welcome to the District of Columbia," Big Mike pulled off and headed home.

TWENTY-FOUR
CAT - 8:00 A.M

CAT HAD A BIG ASS FUNERAL. Almost the whole city showed up to show her some love. V paid for the whole thing, so Cat went out in style.

Bubbles showed up to say goodbye and to tell Cat she was sorry so she could rest in peace. It wasn't a dry eye at the gravesite when they put Cat in the ground.

Black was there to watch her get buried. "Fuck you, Bitch," he spat and walked off. "R.I.P. Cash, Freaky getting kilt next."

HUNTWOOD APARTMENTS

Freaky slept from 1:50a.m. until 2:01p.m. the next day. When he woke up and counted the money, it was 200 bands on the nose. He ordered a pizza and a large Sprite. He ate as he looked over the info Big Mike gave him. Picking up another slice of pizza, he took a bite, and saw Savage's 'Savage Shit' chain. "My young nigga need to wake up ASAP," he said, getting up and putting 50 bands in the cut for when Savage woke up.

Freaky picked up one of the pictures and said, "He's first." The dude's name was Big Russell. He was from up Ivy City, a cold-blooded gangsta and killer. He drove a 2020 Shelby GT Mustang, all white, and he wasn't anybody you could take lightly. Russell was always on point, always strapped up, and didn't trust anybody. But he was on point because it came out that he was hot and been hot for years.

"I'm a flush his hot ass first," Freaky said to himself as he ate another slice of pizza, thinking how he was going to get Russell when Tiana came to his mind. He sat back on the couch, grabbed his phone, and thought *she hip to this shit* as he dialed her number.

―――――

Tiana was getting out the shower when her phone rang. She grabbed it off the sink. Seeing it was Freaky, she answered as she walked to her room ass naked, letting her body air dry.

"Yes, Daddy," she answered.

"You trying to make 10 bands?"

"Hell yeah!" Tiana yelled, thinking about the new heels that she wanted.

"I'll be by to get you around 5:00p.m. Make sure you lookin' sexy as shit and that pussy and ass out." He hung up, ate another slice of pizza and laid back.

SAVAGE

Savage was breathing on his own, and his vitals were better. The doctors said he was doing good, but he just had to wake up. Bubbles hadn't left his side. She didn't go to work or anything. All she did was wash up, change clothes, and sit by his side.

Aunt J and Dawn came by every day, but Bubbles was always by his side praying that he would wake up.

TWENTY-FIVE
FREAKY - 7:02 A.M

FREAKY PICKED TIANA UP, and she looked flat out. She had on a little ass skirt, so short you could see the bottom of her yellow ass cheeks. Tiana didn't have on drawers, and her pretty titties were sitting high in her see-through shirt. You could see her pointy, pink nipples poking through her shirt. Her hair was pinned up, no makeup on her flawless face, and she had on heels that made her walk even nastier.

Freaky rode by Ivy City three times and saw Russell leaning on his car talking to a group of people. He showed Tiana Russell's picture and parked down the block. She leaned over, kissed Freaky on his lips, fixed her titties in her shirt, and hopped out the 650. All eyes were on her as she walked up the block with that nasty walk, signaling everybody to try and holla at her. All of the bitches were watching, sucking their teeth and hating.

"Damn," Russell said to his man as his dick got hard watching Tiana walk up the block. "Aye, shorty," Russell called as she walked pass.

The whole block watched as she stopped, turned, and looked Russell up and down.

"What's up, shorty?" Tiana greeted, smiling, standing bowlegged, watching Russell walk up to her.

"What's your name, shorty?" He asked, examining her from head to toe. *This bitch like that. I got to see what that pussy hitting on.*

"Sexy," she said in a sexy voice. "What's your name, shorty?" She flirted.

"I'm Russell. Fuck you going dressed like that?" He asked, putting game down.

"For real, for real, my dude anything and tonight's my night. I'm trying to get fucked," she said forward, gazing in his eyes.

Russell's dick jumped in his pants. "You fuckin' with me tonight?"

"Do you know how to fuck?" She asked and ran her hand over his dick, seeing that it was hard.

Stepping back, she turned, bent over, and showed him her phat shaved pussy. The whole block went crazy. Russell was geeking. He was trying to fuck right now.

"You think you could handle all this? One night only, daddy. I got a man at home," she said with a serious look on her face.

"Come on," he grabbed her hand, walking to the car. He dapped a few of his men up, then he and Tiana hopped in his car. He pulled off with pussy on his mind. Freaky pulled off behind him with murder on his.

———

Russell fingered Tiana's wet pussy all the way up to H-place. "I'm 'bout to get some drink, I'll be back," he told her as he hopped out of the car and jogged to the liquor store.

Freaky pulled two cars behind Russell's, grabbed his .357, and hopped out of the car. Tiana saw Freaky walk pass and leaned against the side of a building right in front of Russell's car.

Russell brought a 5th of White Remy and some sheets. He was so focused on fucking, thinking with his dick, he wasn't paying attention as he bent the corner. He smiled at Tiana while walking to his car and then he heard footsteps.

Boom!

Freaky pulled the trigger, shooting Russell in the back of his head. He glanced at Tiana, and she had her eyes closed. Freaky's started to kill her too, but he ran off to his car as people came to investigate the shooting. Russell's body shook on the ground.

Tiana was in shock. She had done this before but each time, she couldn't watch. She knew the routine, and she already had her 10 bands, so she chalked it up to the game.

"This the life I chose," she said as sirens got close.

SAVAGE

2 DAYS LATER – 3:08A.M

Savage came out his coma at 3:09 a.m., two days after Freaky killed Russell. Savage's mouth was dry and sore because he still had tubes down his throat and in his dick. He had I.V.'s in his arm giving him fluids. He looked around and saw Bubbles and Aunt J sleeping in chairs by his bed. Then he looked down at his chest. *Where my chain?*

"Fuck is my chain?" He tried to yell but it only came out in a whisper. Looking at Bubbles, still asleep, Savage lifted his arm, grabbed the IV pole, and knocked it over.

Bubbles heard it fall, looked up, and saw Savage staring at her.

"Savageeee!" She screamed, running to his bed, crying as she kissed him on his lips.

Aunt J cried, running out of the room to get the nurse. She thanked God as she cried tears of joy that Savage was alive.

"He's alive!" Aunt J yelled to the nurse and ran back into the room.

The nurse paged the doctor to come and check on Savage

Aunt J pulled out her phone and called Freaky as she watched Bubbles trying to climb in the bed with Savage.

———

"Yeah," Freaky said, answering the phone and looking at the time.

"He's alive, my baby's alive!" Aunt J told Freaky as she watched the doctor checking Savage's vitals and taking the tubes out of his body.

"I'm on my way," Freaky said and hung up.

He got dressed, grabbed his Glock, put it on his hip, and grabbed a Taurus 5th from under his bed. He grabbed Savage's "Savage Shit" chain and left out of the apartment.

———

"Savage, I missed you so much. I haven't been to work or nothing, so you owe me money Lil Boy and some dick. Matter fact, you coming to live with me," Bubbles told him laying in Savage's bed under the covers, staring in his eyes.

"Bubbles, yo shit geeking. Where my chain?" he asked, looking from Bubbles to Aunt J for answers.

"Hey, Baby," Aunt J said.

"What's up, Aunt J. Where my chain at, Moe?" he asked again, looking down at Bubbles, seeing that she was crying.

"You know Cat died at the scene," Bubbles said, looking in his eyes.

"What!?" He couldn't believe his ears, but Bubbles nodded. His head was in disarray, but he was so weak he lacked the energy to morn her properly. *Damn, that's crazy,* he thought. *Not my bitch.*

"I love you, Savage," Bubbles confessed as Freaky walked through the door.

"Y'all in here on some crybaby shit. What the fuck is up?" Freaky asked, smiling and walking up to Savage's bed. "Damn, Bubbles, watch out. You on his dick."

"So what, Freaky!" Bubbles said, rolling her eyes and laid her head on Savage's chest.

Aunt J just shook her head smiling. *That girl crazy.*

"I thought you let one of them wild niggas crush you," Freaky said, dapping Savage up.

"You know I can't die. I'ma Savage," he boasted, looking at Freaky.

Freaky dug in his coat pocket and pulled out Savage's "Savage Shit" chain and handed it to him. Savage looked at his chain, then looked up at Freaky, which Freaky just nodded. Savage didn't even have to ask, he knew Freaky killed whoever took it off his neck. Freaky looked around for the nurse and took the Taurus out of his pocket and handed it to Savage. Bubbles grabbed the Taurus, got out of the bed, put it in her purse, and helped Savage put his chain on.

"Where you get hit, Moe?" Freaky asked, looking at the wrap around his head.

"On the side of my head, the bullet traveled and came out of my neck. I can't die," Savage said laughing.

"Hit me as soon as you get discharged. We got shit to do!" Freaky turned to Aunt J. "You cool, Aunt J? You need a ride?"

"Yeah, I'm tired." Aunt J got up, walked to the bed, and gave Savage a kiss.

"Alright, Moe, hit me," Freaky yelled as he and Aunt J walked out of the room.

"I'm not going nowhere, so get used to it," Bubbles said, laying back down on Savage's chest.

Savage put his arm around Bubbles and closed his eyes. "Rest in Peace, Cat. I'm 'bout to turn the city up!"

TWENTY-SIX
NOOK
SIMPLE CITY - 1:30 P.M.

NOOK HAD JUST COME from the Southside reing up. He pulled up Simp, parked, and hopped out nodding to a few guys as he made his way to his building.

Simple City was on their shit and they wanted work. They were fucked up about Killa getting crushed. Nook heard about it and was Freaky's name in the conversations. He was praying Freaky didn't spank Killa.

As soon as Nook stepped in his building, L stepped from behind the door and smacked Nook in his face with his Glock. Nook fell on the floor, and L put the Glock in his face as L's man, Murder took the gun off Nook's hip.

"Fuck is this about?" Nook asked with his eye slit open, leaking on the hallway floor.

"Your man killed Killa. I know he did it!" L kicked Nook in his face. "You got a week to throw the oop or I'm smoking you and your sister."

L smacked Nook again with the Glock, and they robbed him, leaving him bleeding on the hallway floor. Nook got up holding his bleeding eye.

"Fuckkkk!" he yelled thinking, *this nigga Freaky is out of control!*

SAVAGE - 10 DAYS LATER

Savage got discharged 10 days later. Detectives Rob and Gram came to question him twice. Savage didn't have anything to tell them. Detective Rob didn't speak on it, but his eyes were on the "Savage Shit" chain around Savage's neck.

"That's the same chain that Freaky took off Floyd's dead body," Detective Rob told Gram as they hopped in their unmarked car. "Keep your eyes open. Their asses are going to jail. I'll let them think they're getting away for now."

Savage stayed with Bubbles for another week getting his weight back and fucking. He already had a cool 25 bands and guns in Bubbles' house. He took 15 and brought a 2014 Ford Mustang Boss, black-on-black. He got a fresh fade, and hit the gun store, buying legs for all his dogs. Bubbles bought him a hitting ass Milano sweatsuit, some Jordan 12s, a bust down for his wrist, and some big boy flats for his ears.

"I see you back looking sweet," Freaky said watching Savage sitting on Bubble's bed putting the 30 in his Glock 22.

"You know I'm a Savage," Savage purped as he threw on his "Savage Shit" chain, and put the Glock on his hip.

"That's 50," Freaky said to Savage handing him a bookbag. Savage opened the bag and saw racks, all blue faces.

"It's some info in there too, Slim," Freaky said watching Savage pull out two pictures and look at them. "It's February first, they got to be dead before the month is out. Look at that shit later. I got to go holla at this nigga Gucci about the move, and your man Sky home," Freaky said watching Savage grab the 10 bands out of the bookbag and put it in the closet.

"Kill! That's my work," Savage said as they walked out of the apartment.

"They say you let Cat trick your wild ass into killin' the nigga Cash," Freaky said as they hopped in his 650. "A nigga peeped you the whole time." Freaky shook his head and pulled off. "I got a nigga to throw the oop on Floyd. He had your chain, too. I flushed him, all 5th bullets fucked him around." Freaky laughed. "I'm just waiting on a call. It's three more niggas; Black, Tim, and his bitch ass brother Tom. They on the clock. Shit ain't nothing. But I told yo stupid ass!" Freaky yelled as he stopped at the light. "I was mad as shit you got caught lacking like that. I ain't gon' lecture you but tighten the fuck up with all that tender dick as shit," Freaky told him seriously as he pulled off.

"You right, Slim. my shit was lacking," Savage said, shaking his head thinking about Cat and how he almost didn't make it.

"Shit ain't nothing. You still here. Let's win, fuck these bitches, get this cash and do us like kings till our number gets called." Freaky made a left on 10th Place.

The block was lit, bitches were walking up and down the block in damn near nothing. Niggas was posted in front of buildings, trappin', and blowing gas. Gucci, Shooter, and Sky were sitting on the building steps talking as Freaky and Savage pulled up and parked curbside. Sky was clutching, watching the 650 thinking, *who the fuck is that?*

Savage looked at Sky. *Shorty got big as shit!*

Sky was 5'11", 170 pound brown skin, tatted up, with dreads hanging down to his waist.

Savage hopped out the 650. "You clutchin' and shit, Sky. Fuck is up?"

Sky took his hand off his dog smiling, and walked up to Savage.

"Fuck is up, Moe?" Sky greeted, dapping Savage up.

"Living," Savage replied and introduced Freaky to him. Sky and Freaky dapped each other up.

Freaky stepped off and walked over to Gucci and Shooter. They dapped each other up and walked in the building.

"Slim, you gave me another lifeline," Sky said to Savage as they sat on the steps in front of the building.

"Shit ain't nothin'. Yo wild ass men act like they ain't want you home. I don't fuck with them flatout," Savage told him watching Sky pull out some sheets of gas and twist up.

"I'm already hipped. I crushed Gucci's cousin. The nigga was a rat. They act like they mad bout that. Fuck em doe," Sky said lighting the J. "You cool, Slim, I heard you got hit in the head. I was fucked up bout that situation. Straight up. You look good, Slim. It's like you ain't even get hit," Sky said hitting the J.

"I can't die, Slim. I'm a savage." Savage laughed and watched as two bitches made their way to them.

"Sky who is this?" One of the girls asked looking Savage up and down, liking what she saw.

"Fuck you asking me for? He right here," Sky told her as he blew gas in the air.

"Who is you?" The girl redirected her question to Savage.

Savage looked her up and down. She was 5'3 standing in front of Savage in a pair of leggings looking good as shit. She looked just like

Cassie, same shaved head on one side and everything. The only difference was she was the hood version and was thicker.

"I'm Savage."

"Savage?" She repeated, as she recalled hearing some great things about someone by that name. She looked at his chain and wrist, licked her lips and said, "They call me Me-Me. Give me your phone."

Savage pulled his phone out his pocket and held it out for her to grab. Me-Me looked around, shot a quick glance behind Savage, and grabbed it out his hand.

"You better call too, Savage." She put her number in his phone, handed it back with a seductive look in her eyes, and walked off throwing her ass extra hard, knowing he was watching.

Sky handed Savage the J. "That's Gucci bitch, Me-Me. The other one's name is Dime. I fucked both them bitches as soon as I came home. Gucci always savin' them anything ass bitches," Sky shook his head.

FREAKY - 2:50 P.M.

"I know you been on your shit about Savage getting hit up Woodland," Gucci said to Freaky as they stood in the living room talking.

"Shit wasn't nothin'. Niggas get shot everyday. It's about if they gon' walk it off or lay down and bleed out. You see Savage still walkin' and the other nigga laid down and bled out," Freaky said looking Gucci in his eyes. "What's up with the lick, doe?"

Gucci grinned. "Look, I got some new pictures of the daughter and mother. The mother's name is Amanda and the daughter's name is Tiara. Ain't shit changed. She still drive the Coupe and Tiara still goes to Brown."

"Send me the pictures again."

Gucci grabbed his phone and sent the pictures.

"Alright. I'm on it ASAP." Freaky dapped Gucci and Shooter up and walked out of the apartment.

Gucci looked out the window, then back at Shooter. "What's up with Sky?"

———

When Freaky stepped out the building he looked around to see Savage and Sky sitting on the hood of Sky's Acura blowing gas. "What's up, Slim? You cooling?" Freaky asked walking to his 650. That half a ticket was on his mind.

"Yeah, I'm cool Moe."

"Bet, 28 days, alright Sky," Freaky said and hopped in his 650. He put his 5th on his lap, shut the door, and his phone rang. Answering it, he watched Sky and Savage in the mirror. "Yeah."

"This D-Boy, Slim. Me and Tim going to Popeyes on Naylor Road. Right now, fuck Nook, give me another 5 bands."

5 bands? Freaky thought and grinned. Nook put another 5 bands on top that money. Snake nigga. "Bet, I got you."

"Cool. I got the blue Nationals hat on. Tim got on all red, looking dumb as shit. We about to leave now," D-Boy said and hung up.

Freaky opened his car door. "Ay Savage! Sky!"

"Yeah!" Savage yelled as he and Sky walked to the 650.

"The nigga Tim and D-Boy had something to do with that shit with you and Cat. They on their way to Popeyes on Naylor Road. Tim got on all red. Hit the nigga with the blue Nationals hat on. He was with it," Freaky told them. *Nook bitch ass going be crushed when he find out his cousin got spanked.*

"Bet! I'm wit it." Sky ran to his Acura and hopped in. Savage jumped in the passenger seat, slammed the door shut behind him and Sky did the dash up the block.

Freaky smiled, started the car and pulled off. *Nook a bitch,* he thought.

Sky pulled right in front of Popeyes, spotting Tim and D-Boy in line. Savage's heart sped up, and his adrenaline started rushing as he grabbed the Glock off his hip. He went to hop out when Sky grabbed his arm.

Savage looked back.

"Here, Moe. No face, no case." Sky handed him a black Ski mask.

Savage put it over his face, hopped out the car, and jogged in the store.

"Let me get a 10 piece chicken," Tim ordered and looked confused seeing the cashier's eyes get big, followed by her loud screams.

Boom!

A bullet hit Tim in the head sending blood and brain matter on the counter, register and cashier as she continued to scream. Seated patrons who had been eating ducked for cover. Seeing Tim get slumped, D-Boy took off running out the restaurant. The gunshots echoed in the store.

Boom! Boom! Boom!

Savage stood over Tim's body hitting him. Shells were popping out of the ejection port as Savage pulled the trigger until it decocked. Savage had blacked out.

Blocka!

The sound of a single gunshot brought him back. Blood was all over his clothes. People were in shock, hiding behind chairs and counters. Savage turned and ran out of the store. On the way out, he spotted another dude laid out in the parking lot bleeding out of his chest, a blue Nationals hat lay beside him. Running past him, Savage hopped back in the Acura. People were watching and pointing as Sky pulled off, hearing sirens as soon as he whipped out the parking lot. Sky and Savage looked behind them and saw a police cruiser speeding up on them.

"Bust'em, Moe!" Savage yelled as Sky did the dash, flying down the hill.

"I have a murder suspect in a 2012 Acura LX, tag number 212-566. It's all black, fleeing down Naylor Road. Requesting back up," the officer called in his walkie talkie as he pursued the Acura.

Sky cut up the radio, busting a U-turn in the middle of the street, and flying up the other side of the road, shooting up the hill.

"The suspect's headed back up Naylor Road," the officer screamed into the radio, turning in the middle of the street following the Acura back up the hill.

Savage was holding on to his seat, heart drumming in his chest, as Sky hit the e-brake by *Papa John,* barely missing a car head on. Doing the dash up Branch Avenue, three police cruisers were on them. Sky was in his zone rapping to the Moneybagg Yo, nodding his head.

Savage looked at the side mirror and the police cruiser behind them. He was noid, blood all over his clothes with the murder weapon on his lap. *I ain't going to jail. Fuck that!*

"I'm trending! My shirt, my shoes, my belt this shit comes from Fendi," Sky rapped to the music flying over Anacostia Bridge. He made a left by the graveyard, flying down 17th and Compton, then down Benning road. The streets were blocked off. Sky hit the e-brake sideswiping a police cruiser as he caught the wheel doing the dash board up 21st & I.

"Block all the streets off, all streets!" An officer yelled in his walkie talkie, speeding up behind Sky and bumping the back of the Acura as Sky made a left by the Denny's on Bladenburgs Road. He made a sharp right on 16th street, e-braking and hitting a small alley catching the wheel, leaving a trail of smoke behind him doing numbers down the alley.

Savage looked in the mirror and didn't see a cruiser. "Stop!" Sky slowed the Acura down, they both hopped out of the rolling car and ran up to 16th Street.

Po saw Savage running up the block, and waved them in. Savage saw him and broke to the trap, shutting and locking the door, sliding down the wall looking at Sky out of breath. They heard sirens and the helicopter in the area. Po walked out front, to see police cruisers speeding up the block.

They busted em, Po said to himself.

TWENTY-SEVEN
DETECTIVES ROB & GRAM

"FIRST, we missed Savage getting discharged. He's nowhere to be found, and we have a car outside his aunt's house. Secondly, nobody has any idea where this Freaky motherfucker lives. Third, I know Tim was one of Black's friends. I bet you any amount of money Savage or Freaky did this and why isn't it any fucking cameras focused on the parking lot."

"Fuck, look at this shit!" Detective Rob yelled frustrated as he looked at his partner then around the store, seeing blood everywhere.

SAVAGE & SKY - 7:50 P.M

"Savage, you just got out the fucking hospital and you out killing people, taking the fucking police on a high-speed chase. Shit all over the fucking news!" Bubbles yelled looking at Savage like she wanted to smack him. "And you," she continued her rant, pointing at Sky. "I don't know who you are, but if something happens to mine," she said pointing at Savage, "I'm a kill your ass." She rolled her eyes. "Savage, please stay out of trouble," she pleaded walking up to him and kissing his lips. "I'm going to work. Can you please be home when I get in?"

"I got you," Savage said, palming her soft ass.

"Stay out of trouble," she said and left out of the apartment.

"Bubbles think she own me," Savage said laughing as he walked to the dining room table. He grabbed the J, sat down, and finished counting the 50 bands. Savage counted out 25 bands and slid it to Sky.

Sky looked at the money and then at Savage. *This nigga the reason I'm home and he blessed my game with 25 bands. My own men ain't give me shit.* "Good looking, Moe." Sky dapped Savage up.

"Shit ain't nothing. We in this shit together. Fuck everybody except us and Freaky. Anybody else freepicks!"

"No question!" Sky agreed as he looked at the pictures of the dudes that were on the list.

"We got to crush these niggas, ASAP!"

"I know this nigga," Sky said pointing to an older looking nigga posing in a go-go picture by himself.

"Kill!" Savage said looking at Sky putting the roach in the ashtray. "This the nigga Whiteboy from up Trinidad. Slim, we used to be cool. We used to go on moves together back in the day. He gon' be sweet for it. I just saw the nigga when I came home. He was telling me about a nigga name Tyson that's up, ride around with at least 20 everyday."

"Say no more," Sky said watching Savage get up and walk off to the bathroom. Sky counted his 25 bands again. He grabbed some gas and sheets. *Fuck everybody, even Freaky. I'm only fucking with Savage!*

FREAKY

HUNTWOOD APARTMENTS - 2:00 A.M.

Freaky looked at his watch and saw that it was two in the morning. He grabbed his Taurus, put it in his pocket, and walked out of his apartment. He looked out the hallway building and stepped out not seeing a soul on the streets. Freaky jogged two buildings down, walked to apartment 2, and knocked on the door, putting his back on the wall checking his surroundings. He was about to knock again when he heard the door unlock and crack open a little bit.

"What?" Crackhead Joe asked looking at Freaky.

"You know what the fuck is up?" Freaky said going in his pocket, grabbing $200 and handing it to Joe.

"Alright, hold one second," Joe said closing the door a little bit more.

Freaky opened the door a little bit when Crackhead Joe walked away from it. Freaky peeped in and saw his landlord Mrs. Jones sleeping on the couch ass naked.

Damn, Mrs. Jones get high? And her old ass phat! Freaky thought when Crackhead Joe came back to the door and handed Freaky his truck keys.

"One week, Freaky. Then I got to get back to work," Crackhead Joe stressed. Crackhead Joe was a plumber and had his own truck.

Freaky needed the truck for the lick. "I got you," he said and left out of the building smiling as he walked back home.

NOOK

SIMPLE CITY - 8:00 A.M.

This is D.C. News. Yesterday marks the 70th murder of the year. Yesterday, Tim Jones, age 22, and Donald Boyd, age 20 were gunned down outside of this Popeyes behind me.

"Donald Boyd," Nook repeated as his heart dropped in his stomach. He couldn't believe it when he saw his cousin on the news. "What the fuck!"

Pulling out his phone, he frantically scrolled down his contact list, and called Freaky.

————

At 8:01 a.m. Freaky was parked across the street from Brown Jr. High School in Joe's plumbing truck, eating a bacon, egg, and cheese sandwich. He washed it down with an orange juice, waiting for Amanda to pull up. He looked at his watch and the time read 8:10 a.m. His phone rang, and he looked at his caller I.D. and smiled. It was Nook.

Freaky swiped the green button across the screen to answer. "What's up?"

"Moe, my cousin got crushed yesterday!" Nook yelled tears rolling down his cheeks.

Freaky held the phone to his ear, watching kids walk up to the school. "Let me know when you find out what the fuck going on. You already know I'ma work with you," Freaky said already knowing who killed him.

"Alright, Slim," Nook said and hung up. He called around. He needed answers.

Fuck your cousin, Freaky said to himself and put his phone in his pocket. He looked at his watch and saw it was 8:30 a.m. His eyes were on all the cars and kids walking and parking in the front of the school. He watched as Amanda's car pulled up in front of the school at 8:50 on the dot. The Lex parked and Tiara hopped out, gave her mother a kiss through the window and jogged to the school. Watching Amanda pull off, he threw the food wrappers out of his window and pulled off smiling.

"I got your ass!"

TWENTY-EIGHT

BLACK
WOODLAND - 12:50 P.M.

"DAMN," Black said shaking his head looking over at Tom crying his eyes out about his brother getting crushed.

"I should've went with him, Slim...Fuck!" Tom hopped out the truck.

Black watched him walk up the block. He was lost for words, on high alert. He couldn't believe Tim and D-Boy got fucked over like that. He heard Savage wasn't dead, but he didn't have any info on where the niggas hung so he was really in a hole because they knew where he got money at. He let his mind roam on how he was going to get Savage and Freaky killed when Tyson pulled up beside his truck.

Tyson was Tone's right-hand man, and one of the only people he trusted. He'd never speak his name. Tone just called him the clean-up man. Tyson was a flashy, money-getting, old nigga. You'll never catch him without 20 or better on him. He called himself a walking lick and built his legacy from the ground up. He was a lion. You could feel his presence when he stepped in a room. From the jail cell to the streets, he was a real nigga.

Black grabbed a bag off his backseat, hopped out, and climbed in Tyson's 550. "That's 100," Black said handing Tyson the bag. "Aye, you know a nigga they call Freaky or Savage," Black asked looking at Tyson.

"Freaky naw, but I knew a nigga name Big Savage. But his cruddy ass got crushed a couple of years ago."

"Look I got 50 bands on them niggas head. Let niggas know for me."

"Freaky and Savage, I got you. A black Neon gon' pull up as soon as I pull off. Give us 100 the same way in a month."

Freaky and Savage, 50 bands, Tyson said to himself wondering who the fuck these niggas were as he pulled off.

FREAKY - 1:40 P.M

Freaky had been out all day buying cuffs, zip ties, mouth gags, gasoline, and bleach. He rode around Ivy City to find an abandoned house. He parked, and looked at his watch to see it was 1:43 p.m. Walking in the house, looked around, and nodded his head, liking the space. He put the bleach and gasoline in the abandoned house. Shutting the door on his way out, he walked back to the truck, and hopped in. He was on a mission.

DETECTIVES ROB & GRAM - 1:55 P.M

"We didn't get any prints off the caprice. It was blood on the seats, but it was the victim's blood. The car was registered to an Antonio Keys."

"Antonio Keys," Detective Rob said to himself and looked at Detective Gram. "Stacks, that's Stacks' name. He was killed 8 years ago," Detective Rob said and thought about Sky. He looked at Detective Gram. "Let's find out what's going on with Sky. I heard he just came home," Detective Rob said to his partner as they left out the office.

SKY & SAVAGE - 2:03 P.M

"The nigga drive an all black 550," Whiteboy said as he, Sky, and Savage sat in a chipped-up Dodge Saturn, cruising all Tyson's spots looking for him. Sky drove, Whiteboy was in the passenger seat and Savage was in the backseat. "Turn up 10th, gangsta," Whiteboy said pointing as Sky turned up the hill by the rec. Whiteboy scanned the streets and saw the 550 parked on a side street. "That's him, that's him!" Whiteboy yelled excitedly pointing as Sky rode up the block and made a U-turn. Savage gripped his compact 40 when Sky hit the gas and stopped right on the driver's side door of the 550. Savage hopped out, 40 upped and snatched the door open.

He put the 40 in Tyson's face. Tyson was stuck, pants around his ankles, lacking. He was getting his dick sucked by China.

"Where that shit at?" Savage yelled.

"Don't shoot, Slim," Tyson said looking at Savage's face, mad he got caught with his pants down.

China looked at Savage. *Where do I know him from?*

"Grab that money out of the glove compartment," Tyson told China, happy he always kept a bankroll on him.

Savage took the watch off Tyson's wrist. It was a custom made Patek. He snatched the bag out of China's hand, and back-pedaled to the Saturn, 40 still upped. Savage hopped in and Sky pulled off, flying down the hill.

Tyson shut the door and pulled his pants up. *I'm glad shorty ain't grab me, he could've got damn near an M, rookie ass nigga.* He looked at China as he started the car thinking with his dick again, laughing as he pulled off.

China was still thinking about where she had seen the robber before.

———

"I told you," Whiteboy said as Sky pulled in an alley up E St., parking and wiping down the car.

Savage upped the 40. "Slime you."

Boom!

He pulled the trigger hitting Whiteboy in the back of the head. Whiteboy's head hit the dashboard, blood sprayed all over the windows and seat.

Savage hopped out. He and Sky ran to the Mustang parked around the corner. Savage wiped his face and took off his shirt to wrap the 40 in it. Then he threw it down a sewage drain. Sky took off his shirt that was covered in Whiteboy's blood and threw it down the drain.

Savage gave Sky the watch and they split the 20 bands, 10 apiece as they cruised back up 10th Place.

TWENTY-NINE
FREAKY
BROWN JR. HIGH - 3:45 P.M.

FREAKY WAS PARKED across the street from Brown Jr. High at 3:45 on the dot. He watched Amanda pull up in front of the school and hop out in sky blue jogging pants.

"Damn she phat as shit," he said, watching her walk to the school. She came back out ten minutes later with Tiara. They hopped in the coupe and pulled off. Freaky counted five seconds and pulled off behind her. He followed them to a McDonalds, then to a Walmart. He was going to make his move at the Walmart, but it was too crowded. He followed them to Forrestville, Maryland. They pulled in a CVS parking lot, parked, got out, and walked in the store.

Freaky didn't see anybody in the parking lot as he pulled up beside the coupe, parking beside the passenger door. Freaky pulled his hat low and put his hood over it. He opened the back of the truck, hand on the X-D as he sat in the truck with the door opened a little bit. He watched them walking out of the CVS. As soon as Tiara got to the car, Freaky jumped out and grabbed her, putting the X-D to her head.

"Don't scream or I'm a kill her," Freaky said to Amanda.

Tiara cried looking to her mother for help.

"Walk around the car, now!" Freaky told Amanda as he walked Tiara to the back of the truck.

"Don't hurt her," Amanda cried as Freaky made both of them get in the back of the truck.

With his gun trained on Tiara, he made Amanda cuff herself, then he cuffed Tiara and gagged them both before grabbing Amanda's ass as he shut the door and climbed in the driver's seat.

Amanda looked at Tiara with tears flowing down her eyes. *Why me?*

If only she knew…

DETECTIVES ROB AND GRAM

"Look at this shit," Detective Gram said to his partner as they pulled up 10th Place and saw Sky and Savage sitting on the trunk of the Mustang blowing gas and talking.

"Johnson! Fields!" Detective Rob called them by their last names, hopping out of the car with his gun drawn. "Hands on the hood, now!" He told them as Gram hopped out with his gun drawn.

"Fuck is up?" Sky asked as they put their hands on the trunk of the car. They were happy they put their dogs in the car because the law was geeking.

"When you come home and when the fuck ya'll become so friendly?" Detective Rob asked seeing they were both clean.

"Nice chain, Johnson. I was thinking that belonged to a dead man," Detective Rob said looking in Savage's face. Savage didn't reply but his mind was in overdrive.

"Don't you own an Acura, Fields?" Detective Rob asked. "I know ya'll killed them boys on Naylor Road. I'm on ya'll ass," he said walking back to the car and hopping in. "You get the tag number?"

"I got it," Detective Gram replied as they pulled off.

———

"Fuck that cracker. Call Me-Me and switch-a-roo the bitch," Sky said as they hopped in the car.

"I ain't going to jail. I'm shooting it out first," Savage said seriously and dialed Me-Me's number as he pulled off.

FREAKY - 7:20 P.M

"Noo, ohhhhh Stoppppp!" Amanda screamed as Freaky fucked the shit out of her from the back. Freaky stripped Amanda and Tiara naked and cuffed their hands behind them.

"Damn, this pussy good," Freaky moaned sliding his dick out of her sloppy wet pussy. He grabbed Tiara's face and put his dick in it. "Suck it," he told her and watched her put his dick in her mouth.

Tiara was crying as Freaky held her hair, fucking her mouth. He pulled his dick out of her mouth, pulled her hair, bent her over, and slid his dick deep in her pussy.

"Ohhh!"

"Take this dick," Freaky moaned fucking in and out of her tight pussy. "Fucckkk!" Freaky yelled grinding as he came deep in her pussy.

"Damn, this shit good," Freaky said smiling as he pulled his dick out of Tiara's pussy. He grabbed Amanda's hair and smacked his cum-coated dick on her lips.

He cuffed their feet, got up, and walked to his chair in the middle of the room. He grabbed sheets of gas out his bag on the floor and started twisting up. He watched Amanda and Tiara cry as he looked at their phat pussies and Amanda's body. His dick got hard again.

"This Blaze fault. If ya'll want to live, he gotta pay," Freaky said lighting the J. "I don't know why you crying, your little fast ass wasn't a virgin, anyway. Matter fact, come here."

"Nooo, I'll come!" Amanda pleaded.

"Naw, Tiara...come here, now!" Freaky told her hitting the J stroking his dick with the other hand.

Tiara cried as she walked to Freaky.

"Turn around and sit on it," he told her rubbing her pussy.

Amanda closed her eyes. All she heard was Tiara's moans as she slid up and down on Freaky's dick. She couldn't wait until this nightmare was over.

SAVAGE & SKY - 7:40 P.M

"Yesss, fuck me. Ohhh fuckkk me," Me-Me cried. She was bent over the edge of the couch letting Savage drill her pussy.

Sky had his phone out recording. "Switch-a-roo, vol. 17," Sky yelled putting the camera back on Savage and Me-Me.

"Take this dick," Savage said through clenched teeth.

"Don't stop. Ohhh, I'm cumming. Don't its right here!" Me-Me yelled throwing her ass back, grinning. "Ahhh," she moaned cumming hard, shaking.

Savage came in the condom and pulled out.

Sky handed him the phone, walked up, and put his dick in Me-Me's face. She grabbed it and put it in her mouth, looking in the camera as Savage recorded.

THIRTY
TOM - 10:01 P.M

TOM WAS STRESSING about his brother. He didn't want to be around anybody but bitches. Tom popped 2 perk 10s, and a shitload of Molly. He felt numb as he stepped in Exotics. He got two bottles of Rosé, and ate at a back table, drinking and thinking about his brother. He watched a bad ass, brown-skinned stripper with long dreads pinned on the top of her head come and sit on his lap. She grinded on his dick.

"What's wrong, Daddy?" She whispered in his ear.

The drinks, drugs, and vibe had Tom feeling talkative. "My brother got killed yesterday," he told her as she grinded on his lap, letting him touch her pussy.

"I'm sorry to hear that, Daddy," she replied spreading her legs wider so he could slide his fingers deeper. "You know why it happened," she moaned closing her eyes, feeling her release coming.

Tom knew he was wrong but the drugs and drinks plus the stripper had him so comfortable that he just started talking. "Some bitch ass nigga name Freaky."

Bubbles opened her eyes and came on his fingers thinking *Freaky*.

She turned around straddled him. "Why, Baby?" She sucked his neck, trying to keep him talking.

"Some nigga name Savage and a bitch name Cat did some crazy shit and got handled for it."

"What's your name, Daddy?" She asked, grabbing his hand and walking him to the V.I.P. room.

"I'm Tom," he said as they walked in the V.I.P. room. The only thing that was on Bubbles' mind was letting Savage know and keeping Tom close and comfortable.

FREAKY - 10:20 P.M

"Suck it...Just like that don't stop shitttt," Freaky told Amanda as he closed his eyes and came in her mouth.

Amanda spit his nut on the floor and looked at him with hatred in her eyes.

Tiara was laying on the floor, watching with her pussy coated white with her and Freaky's nut.

"Call 'em," Freaky told Amanda handing her his throw away phone. "He got til tomorrow at 8 in the morning to come up with 600 racks or y'all dead," he told her and watched her dial Blaze' number.

Blaze was uptown in the trap whipping up a brick. He had an 8th left to cook and had just threw some powder on the scale when his phone rang. He wiped his hands, grabbed the phone, and answered. "Hello."

"Baby!" Amanda cried when Freaky snatched the phone out of her hand.

"I got your bitch and daughter. You got til 8 in the morning to come up with 600 bands or I'm killing them. I'ma call back in 2 hours," Freaky told him, hung up, and broke the phone. Freaky walked up to Tiara and turned her on her stomach. Getting in the push-up position, he dipped his dick in and out of her pussy while Amanda watched helplessly, praying that Blaze freed them.

BLAZE

Blaze's heart flopped in his stomach as he panicked. "Fuckkk!" *I only got 250.* "I got to get my daughter!" He yelled as he dialed Gucci's number.

———

Gucci and Shooter were walking out of Denny's, hopping in Gucci's Audi A6 when his phone rang. "This your wild ass man, Blaze," Gucci told Shooter and answered the phone.

"Niggas got Amanda and Tiara, Slim. I need you," Blaze said in a panic.

"Damn, Slim, what you need?" Gucci asked faking like he cared.

"What you got in the cut? I got you, Slim, I need you," Blaze pleaded.

"I'm fucked up. I put my last in your pocket yesterday," Gucci lied.

"Fuck!" Blaze yelled and hung up.

Seeing the call end, Gucci smiled. He had a cool hunnid in the cut.

"Freaky snatched Slim folks," Gucci told Shooter laughing. *The bitch crossed the wrong nigga. Fuck her!*

———

Blaze had to sit down and think. He needed to come up with 600 racks ASAP. He put his head in his hands thinking when Tone and Tyson came to his mind.

"Tone." he said dialing Tyson's number.

———

"Yeah, I let a bitch ass young nigga catch me slipping fucking with the bitch China," Tyson said to Tone laughing when his phone rang. He saw it was Blaze and answered putting it on speaker phone.

"Slim, nigga grabbed Amanda and Tiara. He want 600 racks. All I got is 250 cash. I promise I'll give it back. I need you please," Blaze begged.

Tyson looked at Tone, who mouthed, *we got him, give us 2 hours.*

Tone got up, pulled out his phone, and walked out of the room.

"I got you, Slim. Give me a couple of hours. We gon' get yo folks back ASAP. Just hold tight," Tyson said feeling his pain.

"Good looking. I got you," Blaze told him and hung up. He paced the floor waiting on the call, praying his family was ok.

———

"Damn this a dirty game we playing," Tyson said looking at Tone.

"I'm hipped. Let's get his family back. Then we take it from there," Tone said sitting down thinking, *that could've been any one of us!*

CHINA - 10:50 P.M

China had been watching Bubbles all night, thinking about the guy that fingered her a couple of months ago and wondered if he was the same guy that robbed Tyson. She watched her talking to a light skinned dude all night wondering who he was and though about the type of money Tyson would hit her with if she found out who robbed him. She thought she had an idea and Bubbles was in that conversation.

SKY & SAVAGE - 11:05 P.M

"I told you the bitch Me-Me was a thot. This wild nigga Gucci be fucking all thots. Blaze fucking his old bitch, Amanda. She use to be a thot," Sky told Savage as they sat in the Mustang parked up 10th Place, 2 buildings down from Gucci's building watching them trap.

"That's Shooter, Gucci's right-hand man. Both them niggas snakes," he said pointing and watching them walk in the building. "That's Lil D and Pee Wee." He pointed to two dudes sitting on the steps. "Them niggas yes men, doing anything Gucci tell 'em do."

"Why you be fuckin' with these niggas, anyway?" Savage hit the J. "Them niggas ain't even want you out of jail, Slim. Yo shit lunchin'. I'd be throwin' the oop on all these niggas. Flat out!" He passed Sky the J.

"It's cool. I'll let 'em live. They got one time to play with me, doe. One, Slim and I'ma flush they ass. Pull up my sister joint." Sky crunk up the car and put it in drive.

One time, he thought pulling off.

THIRTY-ONE
FREAKY - 11:31 P.M

"WHAT'S UP, you got the money or what?" Freaky asked Blaze pacing the room naked except for his shoes. Amanda and Tiara were sitting on their knees, cum stains and dried up tears on their faces and bodies. "Yeah, I'ma have it at 12:00. I promise...is my family ok?" Blaze asked.

Freaky walked up to Tiara and put the phone to her ear.

"Daddy!" She cried.

"Tiara!"

Freaky snatched the phone from her ear. "I'ma hit you back at 12."

Hanging up, Freaky threw the phone against the wall, shattering it and causing Amanda and Tiara to jump in fear. He looked at Amanda and Tiara as he grabbed the J from behind his ear.

"This shit almost over." Freaky sat in the chair and got high.

SAVAGE & SKY

LANDOVER, MD – 11:41 P.M.

"I gots to fuck with you, Slim. I don't be really letting niggas know where I lay my head," Sky said to Savage as they parked in front of his building, hopped out, and walked to apartment 6.

"My sister live here too, Slim," Sky let Savage know as he unlocked the front door.

As soon as Savage stepped in the house he saw Sky's sister sitting on the couch in just a pair of thin ass grey shorts and tank top, no socks on her pretty feet. Skin flawless, she wasn't skinny or thick, she was just right and her face was a ten. Sky's sister was beautiful.

"Who is this, Sky?" She got off the couch and stood directly in Savage's face. *His lil ass cute.*

Savage looked at her full lips. "I'm Savage, what's up?" Savage greeted staring in her face.

"Ok, Lil Boy, I'm Beauty and this is my house and my Lil brother," she said pointing at Sky.

"Watch out, Moe," Sky said to Beauty, pushing her out his face.

"Don't do your big sister like that," Beauty yelled watching them walk to Sky's room.

Sky's room was flat out! He had a big 70-inch flat screen on the wall, with the PS5 sitting under it, hooked up to the surround sound system with the wi-fi box sitting on the dresser. He also had a king size bed, on which they sat.

"Beauty shit be geeking." Sky took his 5th off his hip and sat it on the dresser.

Savage sat on the bed and twisted up some gas. Sky cut on the PS5, going on YouTube cutting on all Young Dolph videos and turning it up. Savage took off his shirt, fired up the J, and nodded his head to the music.

Sky walked to the closet, pulled out a duffle bag, and grabbed 2 Drakos out of it. He walked around rapping Dolph. "I got 200 shots on me. I wish a nigga would jump their ass out there. I'm crushing shit." Sky laughed and looked up at the door just as Beauty entered his room.

"What ya'll doing? And give me some," she said standing in the door watching Savage blowing gas in the air with his shirt off.

"Ya'll think ya'll cute," Beauty said looking from Savage to Sky.

Sky sat the Drakos on the bed. "Your shit geeking," he said pulling a knot and handing her a band.

"You, too," she told Savage walking up to him with her hand out.

Savage pulled out a bankroll, counted out a stack, and handed it to her.

"Thank you," she told him and left out of the room.

Savage laid back on the bed getting high thinking Sky's sister was flat out.

FREAKY - 11:50 P.M

"Ohhhhhh," Tiara moaned as she slid up and down on Freaky's dick. Tiara was starting to like how his dick felt in her pussy. She made herself cry whenever she caught eye contact with her mother so she wouldn't know she liked it. "Uhnnnn," she moaned sliding down on Freaky's dick grinding in a circle with her eyes closed feeling good as the pressure built up. "Yesss," she whispered grinding faster as his dick hit her spot. "Ahhhh," she yelled creaming all on Freaky 's dick as Freaky came in her.

Freaky knew she liked it, the way she was fucking him back.

Amanda was mentally drained and dozed off to sleep.

"Suck the nut out of it for me," Freaky whispered in Tiara's ear.

She got off his dick, got on her knees, and sucked it for real this time, knowing her mother was sleep. She sucked his dick good and swallowed all his nut.

Freaky pulled her up by her hair and kissed and sucked on her titties.

"Yesss," Tiara moaned wanting to feel his dick again. Freaky stood up, told Tiara to sit on the floor, and walked up to Amanda to wake her up.

Amanda woke up praying it was a dream.

"Let's see if your husband got the money." Freaky grabbed the phone and called Blaze at 12 on the nose.

———

"Thank you, Slim," Blaze told Tyson as he hopped out the 550 with 350 bands cash.

"Get ya folks," Tyson told him and pulled off. Blaze ran in the house. As soon as he stepped in the house, his phone rang.

"Yeah," he greeted on the first ring.

"You got the money?"

"Yeah, I got it." Blaze grabbed the 250 out the closet and put it with the 350.

"Alright, I'ma call back in 10 minutes with the meeting spot. Any funny shit and I'm crushing both of them." Freaky looked at Amanda, grabbed her by her hair and made her put his soft dick in her mouth. He hung up.

"Suck it," he told Amanda as he dialed Savage's number.

———

"Cut that down, Slim. This Freaky." Savage told Sky as he answered the phone.

"Aye, find a spot ASAP! Nigga gon' meet you with the money. When you get it, flush season. Call me as soon as you get a low-key spot in 10 minutes. We on a clock."

"Bet," Savage told him and hung up.

"Grab the dog. We gone now," Savage told Sky.

They grabbed their Glocks and broke out the house.

BUBBLES

NEW YORK AVE HOTEL - 12:15 A.M.

"You like this pussy, Daddy?" Bubbles moaned as Tom stood between her thighs sucking her clit. She slipped four pills in his bottle and was waiting for it to kick in. She had a cake baked for his ass.

SAVAGE & SKY - 12:20 A.M

Savage and Sky pulled up to Walter place and pulled in an alley behind an abandoned house. They walked in, looked around, and saw that everything was clear.

Savage looked at Sky as he dialed Freaky's phone.

"What's up?" Freaky answered as he sat in the chair smoking, dick hurting, drained, and ready to get the money and get this shit over with.

"Walter Place, house 601," Savage told him.

"If anything look funny, get the fuck out of there."

"Say no more," Savage said and hung up.

———

Freaky called Blaze as soon as he hung up with Savage. Blaze answered on the first ring.

"Walter Place, house 601. My man gon' count it with you. He let me know shit cool, I'ma let your folks go. You got twenty minutes to get there or the deal off. Twenty starts now," Freaky said and hung up.

———

Blaze grabbed the bag and ran out of the house. He threw the bags in the truck and pulled off doing the dash up Walter thinking about his family.

————

Savage stood at the window, watching the streets when he saw headlights and a truck pulling in front of the house. He nodded to Sky and watched a dude hop out of the truck with 2 bags in his hand.

Sky walked behind the door, taking the 5th off his hip, and watched as Savage open the door.

"Let's get this shit over with," Savage told Blaze as he turned around and walked in the house.

Blaze studied Savage's face as he followed him in the house. Blaze was about to shut the door and froze staring down the barrel of a 5th.

Sky pulled the trigger.

Boom!

Blaze's head exploded, spraying the wall with blood and thick chunks of brain matter. His body hit the floor and Sky stood over him.

Boom! Boom!

Sky hit him again. They grabbed the bags, ran out of the back door, jumped in the car, and pulled off.

People in the neighborhood heard the shots, but they minded their business. They were used to people getting killed.

Savage called Freaky and he answered on the first ring. "I got it," Savage told him and hung up.

Freaky looked at Amanda and Tiara and grabbed his 357 out the bag.

Amanda's eyes got big, and she cried and pleaded for her life. Freaky put the .357 to her head and pulled the trigger.

Boom!

Her body hit the floor, blood pouring out her head.

"Nooo! I'll do anything pleaseeee!" Tiara cried and saw a flash.

Boom!

Her body hit the floor.

Freaky cleaned up, got dressed, bleached, and drenched the whole house in gasoline. He lit a match, sat it on Amanda's body and left out the house. Hopping in the car, he drove off and watched the house go up in flames in his rearview.

Lord, forgive me for my sins and the evil that men do fo' the love of money, he said to himself as he headed home.

THIRTY-TWO
FREAKY
HUNTWOOD – 1:29 P.M.

"600 RACKS, NIGGA. BIG BOY LICKS!" Freaky slid Savage 200 bands.

Savage gave Sky 100 out of his cut. They were blowing gas, cooling when Freaky got up and told them he'd be right back.

Jogging to his room, Freaky grabbed his 5th, Joe's truck keys, and left out the apartment. He walked two buildings down, and knocked on Joe's door.

"What?" Crackhead Joe snatched the door open. "Got damn, Freaky. You always showing up so fucking late."

"My fault. Let me use your bathroom, real quick," Freaky said. "I got your keys, too."

"Go 'head. The bathroom to the left in the back," Crackhead Joe said, stepping to the side to let Freaky in.

Freaky walked to the bathroom, taking the 5th out of his pocket. He flushed the toilet with his shirt and walked out of the bathroom.

Crackhead Joe was in the kitchen grabbing a beer, he turned, Freaky put the pistol to his forehead and pulled the trigger.

Boom!

Freaky wiped down everything he touched, laid the key on Crackhead Joe's chest, wiped down the door, and walked out. He threw the 5th on the roof of the building and jogged home. He walked in to find Sky sitting on the living room couch smoking a J. Closing and locking the door behind him, he plopped down on the couch beside Sky.

"Let me hit that."

BUBBLES - 4:40 A.M

Bubbles made sure Tom was out of it, then robbed him for everything. She got her shit and left the hotel, calling Savage as she hopped in her car.

————

"Hello," Savage slurred answering the phone. He looked around to see Sky and Freaky sleep on the floor.

"Hey, Baby," Bubbles greeted in a sad tone sitting in her car outside the hotel room.

"What's wrong?" Savage asked concerned, hearing worry in Bubbles' voice.

"I got a guy named Tom that had something to do with Cat in a hotel room on New York Ave, room 212 drugged."

"Tom?" Savage got up knowing who Tom was as he woke Sky up. "I'm bout to pull up. Go home. I'll see you later and thank you, Bubbles."

"I love you, Savage. Be safe and come home to me," Bubbles said pulling off as she hung up. *I'm sorry I fell in love with Savage, Cat, but you always gon' be my bitch. R.I.P. Baby.*

"Get the money, Moe. The nigga that shot me lacking in a hotel room. I got to crush him," Savage told Sky grabbing his money and waking Freaky up.

"Yeah, Moe?"

"We gone. Tom lacking. Hit my phone."

"Shit better make the news," Freaky slurred, drained, and tired as shit as he dapped Sky up.

Savage and Sky ran out of the apartment and jumped in the Mustang, sitting the money on the backseat as Savage pulled off.

————

Tom only woke up because housekeeping came knocking. He looked around, still dizzy, looking for Bubbles. All of his money and jewelry was gone.

"Dumb ass bitch," he slurred walking out of the hotel room. His car was still at the club. "I did anything," he said to himself as he walked to the bus stop. He was still trying to get himself together and never paid attention to the Mustang speeding his way.

Sky pulled right in front of him, Savage was already out of the car, dog upped, running to Tom.

Tom's eyes got big as Savage pulled the trigger.

Boom! Boom! Boom! Boom! Boom!

Tom's body twitched and jerked as the bullets from Savage's gun hit him from the waist up. Shot after shot, flame sparked from the barrel of Savage's gun until it decocked, chamber and clip empty. He hopped back in the car and Sky smashed out, leaving Tom fucked over at the bus stop.

8:30 A.M

This is D.C. News. Yesterday was a busy day for the district. Police are giving a ten-thousand-dollar reward for any information leading to an arrest for the killers of 14 year-old Tiara Smarts and her mother, Amanda Smarts. Both of their bodies were found in an abandoned house around Ivy City. Both died from gunshot wounds to the head area. Their bodies were so burned, officers were only able to identify them by dental records. Police also found, Chris Smarts, age 34, in an abandoned house around Walter Place, Southeast. Police say this is all connected. Again, a ten-thousand-dollar reward for information. Please contact 1-800-Crimestoppers.

"This shit is fucking crazy!" Detective Rob yelled as he looked around the conference room at the task force gathered. "A fucking 14-year-old girl was killed with her mother last night!" He yelled in frustration. "We found Amanda's car parked in a CVS parking lot. We got the cameras and have footage of Joe's plumbing truck parking beside her car. An unidentified man with a hood on his head held Tiara and Amanda at gun point, forcing them in the back of his truck. The truck is registered to a Joe Clark, age 50, address 5201 Huntwood Apartments, apartment 1. We have surveillance on Joe's apartment and the van. We're going to make an arrest. Let's take this sick motherfucker down!" Detective Rob yelled to his team. He looked over at Gram as they grabbed their coats and ran out of the conference room.

GUCCI - 8:10 A.M

This nigga Freaky a motherfuckin' savage! Gucci said to himself sitting in the bed with Me-Me watching the news. *I'ma get my cut and crush Freaky and his man, fuck that! No ties back to me. That's a triple,* he thought, eyes still on the news.

TYSON & TONE - 8:12 A.M

"What fuckin' part of the game is this. Slim had the fuckin' money. He killed him, his bitch, and their14-year-old daughter. That's some fuckin' savage shit!" Tyson yelled pacing the floor, mad about Tiara getting killed.

"Put the same 350 bands on the motherfuckers that did that shit. Them niggas some suckas," Tone told Tyson shaking his head watching Tyson get on the phone to put out the word.

FREAKY - 8:30 A.M

Freaky was still sleeping when a loud noise from outside woke him up. He got up, still tired and wiping his eyes while walking to the window. He looked out of the window and saw the whole police force setting up in his parking lot.

"Oh, shit!" He yelled in a panic running to his room, flipping the bed and grabbing his Drako. "I ain't going to no fucking jail!"

He cut the news on, heart drumming in his chest as he looked out of the window, watching the police.

———

"We're going in fast and making the arrest. He's armed and dangerous, so be ready," Detective Rob told officers as he put on his vest, grabbed his AR-15, and walked to building 1502.

"The building's been evacuated," Detective Gram told Rob as he walked in the building with ten officers.

"Set up," Detective Gram whispered as he and Rob stepped to the side of the door. He nodded to two officers moving out of the way as they rammed the door, knocking it off the wall.

"Freeze! Freeze!" Officers yelled, running in the house with their guns drawn.

"Clear!" One of the officers called checking all the rooms.

"Damn!" Detective Rob yelled covering his nose, looking down at Joe's dead body and seeing blood all over the kitchen floor and the truck key on his chest.

Freaky's heart rate slowed down watching the police run in Joe's house. He sat the Drako by the door.

I'm glad I crushed Joe ass last night. Best body I ever caught. He smiled and watched the news. *I'm layin' low for a second.*

THIRTY-THREE

TYSON & GUCCI - 12:10 P.M

"THAT'S FUCKED up what happened to Blaze and his family for real, for real, Slim. Any nigga kill a lil girl deserves to die a thousand deaths," Tyson vented as he and Gucci sat in his 550 up 10th Place.

"I'm hipped. Look, this 60." Gucci slid him a book bag.

"Alright, you ever fucked with that dog food?" Tyson watched the mirrors as he slid the money under his seat.

"I been fuckin' with Blaze on that coke."

"Fuck that coke. I'ma give you a brick of dope. Shit take a ten a missile. It sells itself. A car gon' pull up soon as I pull off. Just shoot me 40 bands on the next flip."

"Bet." Gucci was about to hop out of the car when Tyson stopped him. He looked back.

"Aye, you know some niggas name Freaky and Savage?" Tyson's tone was grave. "It's a 50 thousand dollar ticket on their heads."

Gucci sucked his teeth. "Yeah, I know both of them snake ass niggas. I could throw the oop if you want."

"Do that, ASAP! One more thing soldier. It's a big bag on them niggas that killed Blaze and his folks." Tyson's tone was grave. "If ya'll come across a name, you'll be damn near rich."

Gucci looked at him thinking of a lie to tell him so he wouldn't be a part of that shit. "The nigga Freaky came through a couple of days ago. Him and the nigga Savage was asking questions about Blaze. I really didn't pay that shit no mind, even doe I know that's them niggas M.O. But when I saw the news the first thing that came to my mind, I bet you Freaky and Savage did that shit."

"Pull the play. We killin' them niggas." Tyson dapped him up. "A blue Neon bout to pull up. Hit me as soon as you hear from Freaky and Savage."

Gucci hopped out the 550.

Kill two birds with one stone and get rich while I'm doing it, Gucci said to himself, watching the Neon cruise up the block.

Tyson dialed Tone's number as he rode up the street. Tone was sitting on the couch watching ESPN when his phone rang. His lawyer just left after giving him some good news so Tone was in a good mood. "Talk!"

"The nigga Freaky and Savage name keep popping up. Word is they did that to Slim and his folks. I already set the play. I'ma hit you later." Tyson hung up.

Who the fuck is these stupid motherfuckers? Tone thought, shaking his head.

SAVAGE - 12:30 P.M

"That's a hunnid," Savage told Bubbles dropping the last stack in his duffle bag.

"We going out of town, Baby. I want to go down Miami. My brother, Stuntman, live down there. Let's enjoy ourselves for the week-end, pleaseeee," Bubbles begged looking at Savage as she laid on the bed.

"Yeah, we could do that. We driving, doe. I ain't goin' nowhere without the dog on me." Walking to the bed, Savage laid down.

"Okay, Baby." Bubbles crawled to him and laid her head on his chest. "You need to see your aunt too, Savage. Matter fact…" She got out the bed and grabbed her shorts.

"Not right now. I'm hungry and tired as shit. Tomorrow, Moe."

"You promise?" Bubbles asked putting her shorts down, watching Savage.

"I promise. Aye, twist up and fry some chicken, Boo."

"I got you." Bubbles kissed him and walked out the room.

Savage laid back and cut on Menace II Society.

SKY
10TH PLACE – 11:40 P.M.

"Nigga, I'm rich for real. You niggas faking!" Sky yelled hitting his number on the dice. "Nobody move but the money," he told Shooter picking up the money off the ground. They were standing in the alley shooting dice.

"Stop purpin' and shit wild ass nigga. You don't even supposed to be around here anyway," Shooter said looking at Sky.

Sky looked at him confused, hand going to his hip when Shooter busted off on him dropping Sky.

Lil D and Peewee just watched as Shooter took the gun off Sky's hip.

Shooter upped pointing the dog at Sky's face. "Roll out for I smoke your bitch ass!" Shooter yelled watching Sky get up off the ground.

Sky nodded and walked off holding his jaw. "Niggas got me fucked up."

As he trudged up the alley, he dialed Savage's number.

———

Savage blew six J's of cookie, ate all of Bubbles' chicken, fucked the shit out of her, and passed out. Bubbles was sitting on the bed watching T.V. She turned to the dresser seeing Savage's phone ringing. She looked at Savage, kissed his lips, and smiled seeing he was out as she grabbed his phone and answered it.

"Hello?"

"Where Savage? Tell 'em niggas purping. I'm bout to flush something," Sky told her. You could hear the aggression in his voice as he sat in the carryout steaming.

"He," Bubbles said and stopped seeing Sky was serious. "Hold up. Savage." She called shaking him awake.

"What's up, Boo?" Savage slurred looking at her.

"Sky, Baby," Bubbles said handing him the phone.

Savage grabbed the phone, sat up and put it to his ear. "What's up, Moe?"

"Pull up 10th with them sticks out. Niggas round here purping."

"Where you at?" Savage asked getting out of the bed, walking to the closet.

"Up 10th in Yums carryout, hurry up, Moe. Niggas got me fucked up!"

"I'm bout to pull up in like 10 minutes." Savage hung up, got dressed, grabbed the Drako and Mac 11 out the closet and put it in a bag.

"Be safe, please. We going out of town, Savage. I wasn't gon' wake your ass up. Don't make me regret that shit. I'm not fucking playing," Bubbles told him shaking her head and watching him walk out of the room. *I shouldn't have woke his ass up.*

———

Savage pulled up to the carryout, and Sky hopped in the car. His jaw was swollen. Savage didn't speak on it, he grabbed the bag off the backseat and sat it on Sky's lap.

Sky pulled the dogs out the bag, checked the clips, and sat the Mac 11 on Savage's lap as he pulled up 10th Place and parked right in front of Shooter's car. He cut the car off, and they laid back in their seats, eyes on the mirrors waiting. Sky's hand was around the trigger. He was geeking.

———

"You should've just smoked the nigga, Moe. You know Slim gon' be slidin' bout that," Peewee said to Shooter as he, Lil D, and Shooter stood in the hallway of the building.

"Fuck that nigga! He ain't nobody. The nigga a bitch for real," Shooter said watching a junkie walk in the building.

"Let me get a 50, Baby," the junkie said. Lil D served her.

"I'm bout to slide, Slim," Shooter said to Lil D. "What ya'll bout to do?"

"Shit, I'm gone, too," Lil D said looking at Peewee.

"Drop me off up Paris joint," he said as they walked out of the building.

"You did steal the shit out Sky," Lil D said laughing as he walked to the car.

Sky hopped out with the Drako in his hand.

Blocka! Blocka! Blocka! Blocka!

He pulled the trigger, chopping Lil D down. Peewee tried to run behind a car in the street. Savage was up on him, he squeezed, and hit him.

Shooter upped and was hitting back as he ran to the building. Sky chased him down, chopping at him. Bullets were hitting the building's wall, shattering car windows, setting off alarms. A bullet just missed Shooter's head as he ran in the building. Sky hit at the building's door, bullets flew through the door almost hitting Shooter. Shooter laid on the side of the wall watching the bullets hit the steps and mailbox.

Savage stood over Peewee and flushed him. "Let's go, Moe!" Savage yelled to Sky hearing sirens as he hopped in the car.

"Bitch ass nigga!" Sky yelled running by Lil D as he bled out on the sidewalk and hopped in the car.

Savage pulled off doing the dash up the block.

———

"Fuck!" Shooter yelled seeing bullet holes in the walls and the building's door. Car alarms were still going off. He shook his head walking up and seeing Lil D's eyes wide, bleeding out the neck. Peewee was dead.

"Damn!" He yelled and took off running when he heard the sirens close.

The junkie that bought that 50 rock was hiding behind a car the whole time and ran off when the shots stopped thinking, *Sky didn't play no fucking games.*

GUCCI

MONTANA - 3:50 A.M.

"Hello," Gucci greeted, answering the phone. He was up Montana in his cousin Greg's trap, bagging up and cutting the dope with fentanyl making it a missile.

"I knocked your man Sky out, took the dog off him and everything. The nigga came back and flushed Lil D and Peewee, caught us lacking. I spanked back at 'em and got the fuck," Shooter said pulling in front of his house.

"Damn," Gucci said standing up from the table and taking off his mask. "Alright, lay back. I'm pulling Savage and Freaky a move, anyway. Then we crush the nigga Sky. Lay back for a second. I'ma holla at you tomorrow."

"Say no more," Shooter said and hung up as he walked in his house shaking his head. He was fucked up about Lil D and Peewee getting hit. But he thought, *fuck them. Better them, than me. I know one thing, I ain't givin' a nigga a pass no more. If I do something to a nigga, I'm killing him straight up.*

Gucci looked at his cousin mixing the dope as he dialed Sky's number to check his temperature.

———

"This the nigga Gucci right here. Shooter bitch ass got lucky," Sky told Savage as they sat parked out front of Beauty's building smoking.

"Yeah," Sky answered handing Savage the J.

"What's up, Slim?" Gucci greeted.

"Aye, Gucci, I know Shooter yo man and when I catch him, I'm crushing his bitch ass. So, you already know what the fuck is up with me. You with him." Sky hung up and looked over at Savage.

"Me and Freaky gon' spank Gucci, anyway. I got him." Savage handed him the J back.

THIRTY-FOUR
DETECTIVES GRAM & ROB -
10:00 P.M

"THEY FOUND some semen inside of Tiara. We sent it to the lab for testing. Tom got killed yesterday morning. It's like all of Black's friends are dying one by one."

"Ay, Rob," a plain clothes officer called walking in his office. "It was a murder around 10th Place a couple of hours ago. One was shot in the neck. He's out of shock and ready to talk. He's saying something about your man Sky," the officer said smiling.

Detective Rob looked at his partner, grabbed his coat, and left out of the office.

BIG MIKE - 11:01 P.M

"Big Mike, what's up, Soldier?" The Made Man greeted when Big Mike hopped in his truck.

"Same shit, watching the news and seeing the crazy shit that's going on in the city," Big Mike said as he pulled off.

"Yeah, shit been crazy. What's up? It's two more. I don't want to rush you, but I'm tryna get this shit over with. You feel me?"

"I understand. I'ma make sure that shit gets handled."

"Thank you. Now, let's go eat. It's on me," the Made Man said hitting 1-95 headed out of VA.

Mike thought to himself, *why Freaky ain't handle that shit yet?*

FREAKY - 12:52 A.M

Freaky slept all day. When he woke up it was 12:40 a.m. He got up, fired up some gas, and counted all his money. He was at 485 bands, 5 dogs, and a QP of gas. He was going through everything when he saw the pictures of one of the targets Mike gave him.

I wonder if Savage handled that shit yet? He thought as he laid back on the couch. He looked at the info. *I should go handle this shit now, but I'm suppose to be layin' back.*

He debated and said, "Fuck it!" Getting dressed, he threw on all black, grabbed a 17 shot 9, his ski mask, and the info as he opened the door. He froze seeing Pam standing there about to knock.

"Hi, Freaky," Pam greeted in a shy voice.

Freaky looked her up and down, grinned, and looked at her legs in her skirt. "Go 'head in. I'll be back." He hugged her and looked around the hallway as he palmed her ass and kissed her on the lips.

She smiled as she walked in Freaky's apartment and shut the door behind her.

Freaky jogged out of the building, hopped in his car, and looked around as he pulled off.

SAVAGE & SKY - 1:09 A.M

"Who you keep texting, Lil Boy?" Beauty asked looking at Savage from the couch sittin' in some lil ass biker shorts jammed all up in her ass and pussy. Her eyes were low and chinky from the weed, giving her that sexy foreign look.

Savage was laid on the floor sleeping. Too much gas put him down. He looked at Beauty. "Why what's up?"

"Just asking. I'm going to bed. Goodnight, Lil Boy." Beauty stood and looked at Savage while she fixed her shorts pulling them out of her ass and pussy.

Savage stared at her phat pussy print.

Beauty smiled, rolled her eyes at Savage and walked to her room with her ass jiggling. She paused, looked over her shoulder at him, winked, and walked off.

Savage fixed his dick in his pants, looked over at Sky, texted Bubbles good night, and dozed off to sleep.

FREAKY - 1:15 A.M

Freaky pulled up Trinidad and parked by the car lot. Checking the clip of the 9, he looked at the info again, and hopped out of the car. The sky was gray, and it was pouring down raining as Freaky walked up the block. He was looking for a green Lexus. Freaky walked up Bladensburg Road but didn't see the truck. He turned on 16th St, cutting through Denny's parking lot.

He was soaking wet as he walked down the block looking for the truck. He walked by the field and rec, then up Children's Street and spotted the Lex truck. Freaky walked by the field and saw movement in the truck. He put his hand on the 9. Rain continued to pour down, as Freaky crept up to the foggy driver side window. He saw Mook's head laid back on the seat with his eyes closed getting his dick sucked. Freaky upped the 9, tapping on the window.

Mook jumped, his eyes got big.

Freaky saw a man taking Mook's dick out of his mouth.

Boom! Boom! Boom! Boom! Boom!

He pulled the trigger, shattering glass as bullets hit Mook and the faggot. Shells popping out of the ejection port hit the ground until the 9 decocked. Freaky turned and ran up the block.

Mook was from Trinidad, a get money ass nigga. He did ten years and started fucking with boys. He took that shit to the streets. A lot of people didn't know he was on ass but the people that did, knew he had a routine. He'd wait until his wife went to sleep and go out searching. If you found his truck parked at nighttime when the streets were clear, nine times out of ten you were going to find him with a boy. Freaky caught him and flushed him with his dick still out and his lover beside him.

———

Freaky made it home, soaking wet. As soon as he stepped in the house, he took off his clothes. Pam was laid on the couch sleep. He walked up to her naked and kissed her lips.

She woke up grinning with love in her eyes.

"Take a shower with me," Freaky said grabbing her hand and walking to the bathroom.

SAVAGE - 3:31 A.M

Savage woke up and looked around the apartment to see Sky was still sleep on the floor. He stood up and walked to the bathroom to take a piss. After he pissed, he washed his hands and was walking out of the bathroom when he heard, "Savage!"

He looked in Beauty's room and saw her on top of the covers looking at him with her legs in the air fingering her pretty pussy.

"Fuck yesss, Savage," she moaned fingering herself faster looking Savage in his eyes.

Savage's dick was hard, poking through his pants as he watched pussy juice dripping down her thighs. Her pretty nipples standing at attention.

"Ohhhhh shit, I'm cumming ahhhhh!" She screamed and creamed all over her fingers. Her fuck faces had Savage ready to fuck.

"Thank you. Bye, Lil Boy." She smiled and climbed under the covers.

She playing these games, Savage told himself, walking back to the bathroom. He closed his eyes thinking about Beauty, seeing that pussy and beat his dick thinking, *I'ma fuck her*.

DETECTIVES ROB & GRAM

"Peewee died on the scene. I saw him get kilt. I think it was Savage. Sky hopped out with a big ass gun, shooting," Lil D cried as he laid in the hospital bed. Lil D got hit five times; once in the neck, twice in his legs and twice in his chest. The bullets went in and out. He was lucky to be alive. He was scared. He'd never been in a situation like that and had never witnessed someone get killed. It woke him up. Lil D didn't want to die.

"What happened?" Detective Gram asked writing down his statement.

"Shooter and Sky was shootin' dice. They got into it. Shooter knocked him out and took his gun. Sky got up, walked up the block, and two hours later we was walkin' to the car and... Sky and Savage."

"You sure it was Savage?" Detective Gram asked looking at Lil D.

Lil D nodded. "Yeah, it was Savage. He killed Peewee. Sky shot me," he said crying as Detective Gram wrote down his statement.

THIRTY-FIVE
2:02 P.M

GUCCI WAS up Montana with that missile he got from Tyson. He gave out fifty testers. Junkies were lined up from all over the city wanting a test of that dope. He was selling all 20's. He shut shop down at 9 a.m. and told his cousin they were selling all 50 dollar bags. Gucci knew 10th Place was hot, but he had the dope and the plug. He told himself after he pulled this play on Freaky, he was only trappin' up Montana. Fuck 10th Place.

Gucci was sitting in the trap watching his cousin Greg and two of his men, Lil Andy and Pat, weigh out ounces of dope. The heroin was so potent you had to have a mask on. Gucci called Tyson early that morning, and grabbed his last 40 racks, plus the 20 bands he had made today. He still had 28 ounces left from the first brick. He called Tyson to get another one. He already knew that shit was up and down.

Gucci was looking out the window, watching Tyson pull up in the parking lot. He grabbed the 60 off the table and was leaving out of the apartment when his phone rang.

"I'm walking out now." He hung up, jogged to Tyson's car, hopped in and slid Tyson the 60. "I want another one. It's 20 to the next bill in the bag, too."

"Alright." Tyson slid the bag under his seat. "What's up with that shit we talked about? I don't want them niggas walking this earth no more."

"I'ma set that shit up today, Slim, ASAP!"

Tyson checked the side and rearview mirror. "Alright, same routine. A black Taurus gon' pull up as soon as I pull off."

"Bet!" Gucci hopped out the car.

Watching the Taurus pull in the parking lot, he told himself that he would call Freaky as soon as he got in the trap.

BLACK - 5:10 P.M

Black was trappin' good, but he was sticking and moving. Paying traps, switching spots on high alert, hand always on his dog. He was paranoid. Thinking he was dying next, he wasn't going for that. He red up early in the morning. He had an ounce sell Uptown for 3600. Bagging it up, he wrapped it and left out the trap. Black hopped in his car and pulled off, dog on his lap, eyes on the mirrors. He rode down Naylor Road and saw lights flashing in his rearview.

"Shit!" He put the dog and ounce of dope in the glove compartment at the officer's signal for him to pull over.

Black thought about running. He'd just got off papers, and knew a gun and an ounce of dope would sit him down for years. He took a deep breath, said a quick prayer, and pulled to the side of the road. Detectives Rob and Gram pulled behind him and hopped out with their guns drawn, walking up to his car.

"What's the problem?" Black asked as Detective Gram opened his door and ordered him to step out of the car.

Black put his hands up and stepped out of the car. "What's this about?"

Gram made Black put his hands on the hood and searched him, as Detective Rob searched the car.

"Cuff 'em," Detective Rob told Gram holding up a gun and ounce of dope in the air.

"Fuck!" Black shook his head as they escorted him to the car.

FREAKY - 6:02 P.M

"Are you going be my boyfriend or naw?" Pam asked laying on Freaky's chest, smiling in his face.

Freaky was palming her ass, kissing her neck when his phone rung. "Get that," he told her and smacked her ass.

Pam climbed off Freaky in just her thong and walked to grab his phone off the table. She grabbed it and walked back to him with her thong string between her pussy lips.

She handed him the phone and climbed back on his body. Freaky palmed her ass as he answered the phone. "Yo."

"What's up, Slim?" Gucci greeted.

"Same shit. The move went sweet," Freaky said talking about the move as he pushed Pam's thong to the side and slid his finger in and out of her pussy.

"When you pullin' up?" Gucci looked over his shoulder at Shooter.

"I'ma pull up tonight. I'll call around 8 p.m. when the sun go down."

"Say no more." Gucci hung up, smiled at Shooter, and called Tyson to put the play in motion.

Freaky kissed Pam on her lips and pulled his finger out of her wet pussy. He sucked her juices off his fingers and dialed Savage's number.

———

"Bout time you came to see an old woman. I missed you Savage," Aunt J told Savage with tears rolling down her face as she hugged him.

Bubbles leaned on the wall, smiling, face streaked with tears as well. She was happy watching Savage hug Aunt J back.

"You know I love you, Aunt J." Savage wiped her face.

"Enough crying', nigga," Aunt J stepped out of his embrace and looked at him. "Give me some money for me and for the rent."

Bubbles and Savage laughed, and he went in his pocket and handed her a bankroll.

"What's this?" She asked excitedly and counted the money.

"4 bands."

"Thank you, Savage. That's why I love you. You always looking out for Aunt J," she said leaning toward Savage, kissing his cheek.

Bubbles grinned as she walked up to Aunt J and gave her a hug.

Savage grabbed his phone out of his pocket and answered it as he sat on the couch.

———

"What's up, Moe? That Gucci situation is tonight. I'ma pull up and get you in an hour. Flush this nigga tonight."

"Say no more," Savage told Freaky and hung up.

———

Freaky dropped the phone, got up, and pulled Pam's thong off. He spread her legs and licked and sucked her clit.

"Freaky, I love you," Pam moaned with her eyes closed, grinding on his face.

Freaky pushed her legs back by her head and licked from her pussy too her ass, tongue fucking her asshole.

"Ohhhh, I'm cumming," she yelled with her body shaking thinking, *Freaky's my dude forever!*

BLACK - 6:40 P.M

The detectives had Black sitting in the interrogation room for the last 40 minutes. His mind was racing. He had 130 bands in the house and a baby on the way. He was winning and wasn't trying to do anymore jail time at all.

Detective Rob walked in the room with a Ziplock bag containing the gun and dope. He sat it on the table in front of Black, who looked at it, then back up at the detective.

"All your friends are dead. Cash, Floyd, Tim, Tom, and you're next!" Detective Rob barked, pacing the room. "Now, the gun and dope...with your record, you're going to cop to at least 25 years and that's if you're lucky. I could make all this shit disappear right now, but I need you to help me. I'ma give you five minutes to think about it." Detective Rob grabbed the Ziplock bag and walked out of the room.

"Shit!" Black laid his head on the table. *I ain't no snitch,* he thought, mind on everything Detective Rob said. *But I can't do no jail time!* "Damn, I'm in a jam."

Detective Rob and Gram were watching Black from behind the two-way mirror.

"We got 'em," Detective Gram told Rob as they watched Black sweat.

"Let's see," Detective Rob said walking from the room, with Gram following close behind. He walked to the interrogation room and stepped in. "Five minutes up!"

Black raised his head off the table and looked up at the detectives. "So, if I help you, I could walk out the door right now, today."

"That's what I said," Detective Rob replied.

Black took a deep breath and looked at the detective, thinking, *I'm doing anything.* "What's up?"

I got his ass, Detective Rob thought. "Who killed Cash? And what happened with Cat and Savage?"

"Savage smoked Cash and Cat set the shit up. Floyd caught 'em lackin', kilt Cat and shot Savage," Black told the detective putting Cat's murder on a dead man.

"Did Floyd take Savage's chain off his neck? The one that says Savage shit?"

"Yeah."

"Who kilt Floyd?" Detective Rob asked.

"It had to be Freaky, but I wasn't there so I really don't know." Black looked around the room. *I can't believe I'm doing this hot ass shit!*

"I got one more question for you. I know you heard about the case the Feds are building and a lot of people are popping up dead. So, I need to know…that heroin we found in your car, who you get it from?" Detective Rob asked looking Black in his eyes.

Black stared back at him. *I ain't tellin' on Tone or Tyson…fuck that!* "A nigga came from out New York."

"Alright, I'ma make this disappear and get you some papers to sign. You're free to go after that, but you're going to help us out every now and then." Detective Rob grinned and walked out the room.

"Damn!" Black let out, mad as shit as himself, and his laid his head on the table.

THIRTY-SIX
SAVAGE & FREAKY - 9:10 P.M

10TH PLACE WAS DEAD. It wasn't a soul on the block. The yellow tape and chalk lines were still in the street from Pee-wee's dead body.

Gucci stood in the trap, looking out the blinds, waiting for Freaky and Savage to pull up. He already called Tyson and let him know they were on their way.

Tyson sent a killer that was parked down the block waiting for the green light.

———

"Look, let the wild niggas get close to the car, then crush they ass," Freaky told Savage as they pulled up 10th Place.

Savage opened the passenger door a little bit but held it to make it look like it was closed with his left hand. The 5th was in his right hand, his finger on the trigger, geeking.

———

Gucci watched them pull up. He made the call to Tyson's killer, hung up, and put the Glock behind his back as he stepped out of the apartment.

Freaky was about to call him but put his phone back in his pocket when he saw Gucci walking out of the building.

Savage watched Gucci as he walked closer. "Fuck he got his hand behind his back for?"

Gucci looked in Savage's eyes, feeling funny.

"That's a dog!" Savage yelled and pushed opened the door and got to clickin'.

Boom! Boom! Boom! Boom!

Feeling a bullet graze his face, Gucci upped and got to clickin' back.

Boom! Boom! Boom!

Bullets hit the back door and Savage shut the passenger door as Freaky pulled off.

A car pulled right up to Freaky's window, Freaky turned and saw a gun in his face. Freaky ducked, pushing Savage's head down as the killer pulled the trigger.

Blocka! Blocka! Blocka!

Glass shattered and fell on Freaky as he smashed out.

Gucci ran in the street still clickin'.

Boom! Boom! Boom!

Bullets shattered the back window as Freaky did the dash up the block.

Gucci and the killer caught eye contact, Gucci nodded and ran off to his car.

I know I hit one of them niggas! The killer thought as he pulled off.

———

"Bitch ass niggas!" Savage yelled as they pulled in an alley wiping the car down.

Freaky popped the ignition to make it look stolen. He took off the tags, threw them on a roof, and looked at Savage. "I'ma kill that nigga!"

They ran up the street, pulling out their phones, thinking the same thing. *I ain't letting them niggas breathe.*

BLACK - 9:15 P.M

Detective Rob and Black walked out the police station. "You want me to give you a ride to your car?" Detective Rob asked.

"Naw, I'm cool," Black was trying to get the fuck away from the station.

"Alright, be safe," Detective Rob said sticking out his hand.

In a hurry to get away from the police, Black didn't think when he stuck his hand out and shook Detective Rob's hand. Ending the hand-shake, he gave the scene a once over. Satisfied that he was leaving unnoticed, he walked to the bus stop.

———

"You saw that shit?" Tyson asked his little cousin Keem as they sat at the light watching Black walking out of the police station and shake a detective's hand.

"Yeah, fuck he a rat?" Keem asked, hand going straight to his waist.

Keem was from the Southside. He was 24 years old and already had 10 bodies under his belt. He was an impulsive, violence-loving young nigga that was trying to kill and work.

That was his M.O., a workhorse.

The light turned green and Tyson pulled off and turned in a gas station right across the street from the bus stop to watch Black while he called Tone.

———

"One more to go," Tone said to himself when his phone started ringing. He grabbed it and saw it was Tyson calling. Tone was hoping that Tyson was calling to tell him the little dudes Savage and Freaky were dead. He answered. "What's up?"

"Aye, I just saw your man Black coming out the police station shaking the police hand. What's up? I got Keem with me?"

Tone didn't say anything for a couple of seconds. His first thoughts were that *Black might have a good reason*, then all the shit he was going through popped into his head. "Handle that. I ain't takin' no chances. Give Keem 15 bands when it's done."

Tone hung up and Tyson looked over at Keem. "I got 15 bands for you. I'm bout to pull up the block."

"Alright," Keem said geeking as he hopped out of the car.

Tyson pulled off and drove up the block.

Keem circled the block looking around for the police as he walked to the bus stop.

Black was the only person at the stop. He was in his own world, praying nobody found out he was talking to the police.

Keem walked up, nodded to Black, and sat on the bench behind him. He slid the dog off his waist, looked around, and didn't see anybody. Putting his finger on the trigger, he stood up and upped the dog. "Ay, Holmes!"

Black turned towards the voice.

Boom!

The bullet tore through his skull, and Black's body crumbled to the floor beneath him.

Boom! Boom!

Keem hit him again and broke up the block to the car, conscious of the fact that he had just caught his 11th body.

———

Detective Rob and a couple of officers heard the shots and ran out of the police station with their guns drawn. They got to the bus stop and saw Black on the sidewalk with his brains hanging out of his head.

"Shit!" Detective Rob lowered his firearm and kicked air. He looked at Gram and he slowly shook his head. Rob pulled his walkie-talkie off his waist and brought it to his mouth. "We need a medic!"

THIRTY-SEVEN
SKY

SKY DROPPED 35 bands on an all-platinum Cartier watch, and dropped another 30 bands on a 2016 Tahoe, black on black, with tinted out factories still on it. He got his hair done in a crown and had the P90 on him with the 36 in it sitting on his lap. Dior down, in some skinny Zara jeans and Dior boots on his feet. Big ass diamonds in his ears, platinum shit. He had 10 bands on him, cruising Uptown when his phone started ringing. He cut the music down and picked up the phone.

"What's up, Moe?" Savage greeted sitting on the couch watching Bubbles put 50 bands in her bag.

"Shit, coolin'. Fuck happened with the nigga Gucci?" Sky pulled in McDonalds's parking lot across the street from Howard University.

"The nigga was tryin' to pull us a move. I got to clickin' at 'em. Some nigga pulled up on the side of the car hittin' and almost crushed me and Freaky. Freaky mad as shit. I can't wait to catch the nigga." Savage grinned.

"Damn, we gon' crush his scared ass. That scared ass nigga hidin' and shit." Sky watched his surroundings. "I should've pulled them a move that night we was sittin' on the block watchin' them. They was lackin', too."

"Look, Slim, me and Bubbles bout to slide out of town for a couple days. She geekin'."

"Boy, don't make me smack you, Savage!" Bubbles rolled her eyes at Savage with her hands on her hips. Sky laughed.

"I need you to handle that last situation for me too, Slim," Savage told Sky as he handed the J to Bubbles.

"I got you. Shit a be done before you get back to the city."

"Bet! Be easy, Slim. Don't let none of these niggas catch you lacking." Savage stood and grabbed the bag with the money.

Bubbles grabbed his compact 5th off the dresser and put it on his hip.

"Love you, Slim. I'm gone." Savage hung up and followed Bubbles out the house.

"Me, lacking?" Sky cut the music up and pulled off. "You know I ain't lettin' none of these wild niggas trick me. You know I do the trickin' niggas and shit. Stop playin' so much." Sky laughed and checked his rearview mirror.

FREAKY – 2:10 P.M

Freaky bought a low key 2010 Dodge Magnum, all black with dark tints. He had the one switch. He was on his shit looking for Gucci. He slid up 10th Place and saw a police cruiser sitting by the building with the big light sitting on the side of the street.

"Bitch ass nigga hidin'. I'ma catch his ass." Freaky cruised up the block pass the police. "I'ma pull up on Nook's bitch ass. Hopefully he ain't there so I can fuck his lil sister." He smiled thinking about that good young pussy as he hit Benning Road.

———

Freaky pulled up Simple City, parked and hopped out. He felt a funny vibe seeing people speed walking in buildings and cuts. It was quiet as he closed his door with the 18 still in his hand. He nodded to a few people, when he saw L, Rocky, and Lil 40 running out of the building with fully shit in their hands.

Freaky started backpedaling, upping as L started chopping.
Blocka! Blocka! Blocka! Blocka!
Bullets flew at Freaky and he hit back. Again and again, he

squeezed the trigger, letting off shots until he felt a hot bullet rip through his shoulder, spinning him.

"Ahhhh, fuck!" Freaky ducked low and crawled to his car. He could feel the blood running down his arm as bullets continued to rain in his direction. Shots fired and ricocheted off his car, trees, and the surrounding buildings. Reaching his car, he heard the approaching footsteps as he climbed in. Lil 40 was just turning the corner. Freaky upped and flushed him.

Blocka! Blocka! Blocka! Blocka!

Bullets hit him in his neck and chest and Lil 40 fell on the back of his head in the middle of the street.

"Fuck!" L yelled seeing 40 laid out and started running down the street with the Mac 11, lighting up the whole street.

Freaky let off the whole 50 as he hopped in the car.

L and Rocky ducked behind a car. Freaky's arm was gushing blood, heart racing as he started the car. People were in buildings, windows, and sidewalks watching as Freaky pulled off fishtailing. L and Rocky ran from behind the car, chasing Freaky's car down lettin' off shots.

The back window shattered, bullets hit Freaky in his arm and the back of his neck, as he e-braked at the corner doing the dash down the hill.

L and Rocky looked at Lil 40's dead body and took off running from the scene.

Freaky was seeing double. He was losing too much blood. He flew down the hill, ran the light, and crashed into another car head on. The gun dropped on the floor as Freaky blacked out.

DETECTIVES ROB & GRAM

"The DNA still hasn't come back on Tiara yet," Detective Rob told Gram as they sat in their office going over their notes. "I don't want to put an arrest warrant on Savage and Sky yet. Lil D's going to be a good witness but I want to get them on more. We still don't have shit on Freaky except the liquor store incident, and we can't identify him from the video," Detective Rob stressed when a plain clothes officer came in the office and told him that his man Freaky was on the news.

"Yeah?" Detective Rob yelled excitedly looking at Gram as he cut on the T.V. and turned to the news. He turned the volume up.

This is D.C. News. We stand here up Simple City where a big shootout happened at 2 p.m. today. James Pose, age 17, was killed in the middle of the street from a gun battle. Damian Jones, age 24, was shot in the neck, arm, and shoulder. He was also involved in a car crash that left him unconscious. He's in I.C.U. at this time. Officers found a gun in his possession that was used to kill James Pose. He has been arrested and officers are waiting until he comes out of his coma.

"Oh shit!" Detective Rob yelled smiling at his partner. "We got 'em," he said as they got up, grabbed their coats, and walked out of the office.

GUCCI & SHOOTER

"You see that shit?" Gucci asked Shooter watching Freaky's face flash across the news screen.

"I hope the bitch ass nigga die," Shooter said as Gucci dialed Tyson's number.

TYSON

"What's up?" Tyson answered the phone. He was in the office at Exotics getting his dick sucked by China.

"Cut on the news, Slim. The nigga Freaky just got hit. His shit all over the news. They arrested him for a joint! His name is Damian Jones. Cut on the news." Gucci hung up.

"Hold up," Tyson told China pulling his dick out of her mouth. China got up off her knees. Tyson smacked her ass and put is dick in his pants. He cut on the news as he dialed Tone's number.

"Big bamma ass nigga," Tyson said looking at Freaky's face when Tone picked up. "Turn to the news, Slim. Your man Freaky on it. He killed some young nigga and got hit. They probably charged him for the body. He in a coma in ICU right now. I hope his sucka ass die," Tyson said looking at Freaky's face flashing across the screen.

"Damian Jones?" Tone looked at Freaky's face.

"Yeah, that's that sucka," Tyson said, eyes locked with China as she played with her pussy.

"Bob from up third and Budda still up the jail?" Tone asked.

"Yeah, I just sent them niggas a couple grams over there."

"Let them know it's a ticket on the nigga head. Crush his ass ASAP, if he come over there."

"Say no more," Tyson said hanging up. He pulled his dick back out of his pants looking at China as she walked up to him grinning.

SKY

Sky was parked in front of Big V's house in a chipped-up Dodge Intrepid, dressed in all black, Drako with him, waiting.

Big V had been getting money since the 90s, but he never did a day in jail. Niggas had a feeling he was a rat, but no one saw no paperwork or knew who he told on. The nigga face sells. He'd been around so long he knew everybody and could get his hands on anything. The Made Man's lawyer found out why his name was never in paperwork and most niggas take cops so he never had to get on the stand, but the Made Man found out the truth.

He wanted Big V dead. The Made Man had just sold him a brick of dope personally. The Made Man needed him dead! Big V didn't think anybody knew he was working. He'd been ratting so long and no one found out yet. Even with everybody on the case dying, he still didn't think niggas was hipped to him.

Big V and the Made Man had just talked. He made sure Big V was comfortable. He didn't know it was a ticket on his head and Sky was parked in front of his house, lurking. So, when Big V pulled up at home, he didn't check his surroundings. He didn't have a care in the world til he saw a dude running up on him with a big ass gun in his hands.

Big V tried to block his face with his hands. Sky upped and put 50 bullets in him. When police responded to the scene, they found Big V's dead body laid out by his car, bleeding out, eyes still open.

Big V died with 50 bullets in him and a wire still taped to his chest.

THIRTY-EIGHT
SAVAGE

SAVAGE AND BUBBLES didn't get to Miami until 3 a.m. As soon as they hit the hotel room, they laid down and went out. The next day was a beautiful, sunny day with clear skies except for the thin wisps of clouds here and there. Bubbles took him sight-seeing. She took him around Back Blues, up 131, and Portland Road. There were bitches everywhere. They stopped by a candy lady named Mami and got plates of Salmon patties and eggs. Bubbles took him up 61st and 13th Ave, and bought a QP of some cookie. The shit was so strong, by the time they pulled up Saks, Savage and Bubbles were high as shit.

They dropped 20 bands in Saks. Savage got all Versace shades, belts, and shoes. Bubbles got herself all Gucci. They got back to the hotel around 9 and got fly. Savage took ten bands with him to the club. They hit Club LV, and got the VIP on the balcony. Ten bottles with the sparkles came to their section.

Lil Baby blasted out of the speakers. Bubbles danced on Savage as he drunk Rosé out of the bottle. He had the 5th on him looking sweet. Bubbles looked at Savage with love in her eyes as she grabbed the bottle. They were both standing on the couches. Savage handed Bubbles the rest of the money, gave her a kiss, palmed her ass, and told her to throw that shit as he looked over the balcony drinking out of the bottle.

Bubbles grinned and threw the money. Bitches were looking at Savage and wondering who the fuck he was. Niggas were looking too, while hating ass bitches were fighting for the money.

Savage matched the stares of the niggas; mugging, purping.

Bubbles grabbed his face, kissed him, and smiled. *I love this nigga!*

They partied all night.

TIANA

TIANA AND KEYSHIA went out ATL to a *Future* concert. They met a nigga named Big Bag that was willing to pay them a band a piece for some head and pussy. They both were with it, plus they brought some date rape pills with them that would put him down.

Big Bag was a major player in the A. He scammed and was up. They pulled up to the hotel and Tiana looked at all Big Bag's jewelry and his stuffed pockets. She was plotting.

When they got to the room, they began drinking and blowing gas. Keyshia started sucking his dick as he snorted a line of powder off Tiana's titties. He grabbed the Rosé to wash it down.

He didn't know Tiana dropped a couple of pills in his bottle until he started fucking Tiana and felt dizzy. Once he passed out, Tiana and Keyshia robbed him blind and left him. The housekeeper came the next day and found Big Bag in the bed, dead with blood all over his face.

The Police did an investigation and found out he was drugged. They rewound the tapes and saw Tiana and Keyshia hurrying out of the room with the jewelry in their hands. The detective had seen this too many times. He found out who Tiana and Keyshia were and issued a warrant for their arrests.

They arrested 4 days later in Washington, D.C., shopping in Saks, swiping fake I.D.s. They stayed at CTF for a month, then were transferred to Atlanta. They were both charged with Robbery and Second-Degree Murder for Danny Stanly AKA Big Bag.

Tiana cried her eyes out. "I can't do no time." Her lawyer got her in touch with the District Attorney, and they set up a meeting.

As soon as Tiana stepped in the room, she told the District Attorney she had witnessed a murder and was willing to testify if she could go home.

TO BE CONTINUED...

Stuck In The Trenches 2
Coming Soon

Did you enjoy the read?

Let us know how much by leaving us a review on Amazon and
Goodreads.

KEEP READING FOR A
PREVIEW OF...

Ridin' For You
By Telia Teanna

CHAPTER ONE

"Shit, I gotta answer this." Zyair put his long-tattooed index finger to his lips, quietly shh-ing her.

McKenzie looked up at him with amused eyes and opened her mouth wider, taking more of his thick dick into her mouth. His lips parted and his hips slightly thrusted up into her mouth.

He was naked from the waist down. His onyx skin caused her mouth to water with the way that the sun shined through the large floor to ceiling windows of the condo he bought her recently.

"Wassup, baby?"

From her knees McKenzie's eyes shined bright with mischief as she watched her fuck buddy try not to moan while he was on the phone with his fiancée. She could hear her on the other side ask him where he was, so she purposely gagged on his dick, making him inhale sharply.

"Oh shit," he mumbled under his breath, tangling a big hand in the expensive Peruvian bundles that he had bought her also.

"Nothin'. I'm just taking a shit."

McKenzie choked on his dick because she laughed. This nigga ain't shit. She was laughing on the inside. Only a dumb bitch would believe some shit like that. Niggas don't take shit outside their houses.

He bit his lip and nodded down at McKenzie, humor lighting up his normally empty eyes. He knew that she always got off on doing nasty shit to him while he was on the phone with his bitch.

He'd be a lying ass nigga if he said that he never planned some of the calls between them. Her pussy was soaking wet every time. Even at that moment he knew she was enjoying every moment of him being on the phone while she sucked him off. She was playing with that little wet pussy, and it only made him grow harder in her mouth.

"How was your day, babe?" He asked. He knew that if he asked, she was going to talk his ear off for the next twenty minutes before asking if he was paying attention.

"Weeeell, I went to the mall today, right?" He muted his mic and dropped it on the couch.

"I'm funny to you, huh?" McKenzie's bronze eyes met his almost black ones and winked at him, taking his long dick down her throat, swallowing him.

"Fuuuuuck," he moaned, sinking further into the couch and spreading his legs wider apart.

That trick right there was the very reason why he could never leave her ass alone. He couldn't imagine a life where he couldn't get his whole dick swallowed the way she did it. No other bitch had been able to do so, and he doubted that another bitch could.

"Mmmm," she moaned around his shaft when he tangled both his hands in her hair and thrusted in and out of her throat, moaning loudly.

That was another thing that was special about McKenzie, she was with whatever pleased him sexually. She basically let him use her as his personal fuck doll.

Yes, he had a whole girl at home that he was going to be marrying in just a few months, but there was no fucking way that he could exist in life without McKenzie's sex. She was the only one that could ever completely satiate him. And truthfully, he didn't care that he had a woman that worshipped the ground that he walked on at home.

The two could have made the perfect couple, but McKenzie didn't want to be tied down.

He groaned. "Fuck, I love this throat." He licked his lips and removed his hands from her head to let her breath.

The way his wet dick slid out of her throat and she looked up at him with "fuck me" eyes and for a second, he lost his train of thought and saw nothing but her.

"Better answer her." Her sultry voice broke him from his trance.

McKenzie chuckled and slapped his big black dick against her tongue. She loved the attention and intensity that he gave her when she was making him feel good. She didn't know why but she loved sucking Zyair's dick so much, that sometimes she'd meet up with him when he was out in the field just so that she could get a taste of him and hear him moan her name.

She was his fucking weakness and she knew it. It was one of the many perks of having a baller ass nigga like Zy. His fire ass pipe game was another perk. Her favorite perk.

He picked up the phone and unmuted it. "What you say, babe?"

"I asked what kind of flowers did you think that we should get for the wedding?"

Her question immediately irritated him. He didn't fucking know, nor did he care. He was busy trying to buss a nut down his side bitch's throat.

"You know I don't knoooow-" he drew out the words at the exact moment McKenzie released his dick from her mouth, lifted his balls and one of his legs, and licked his gooch.

"What the heck are you doing?"

He couldn't mask the moans that left him as she teased the sensitive space between his anus and balls.

McKenzie laughed against his flesh when she heard his girl going off.

"You're with that bitch, aren't you?" She was livid.

McKenzie pulled away from him and laughed out loud. "He is, hoe. Now get the fuck off the phone so I can finish eating our nigga's ass, bitch," she taunted her.

"Zyair! You just gonna-" He hung up the phone.

"You always gotta fuckin' start some shit, Kenzie. Why you ain't just be quiet?" He huffed annoyed. He didn't feel like arguing with his bitch when he got home.

"'Cause I ain't feel like it." She winked at him and lowered herself onto her hands and knees. "Now, scoot down."

She didn't dare reach out to pull him further off the couch so she could reach her designation easier, he always threw a fit when she did. He'd go off on a rant talking about him being a grown ass man and not to handle him like he was some kind of bitch.

"I'ma stop fuckin' with you one day, I swear." He adjusted himself on the couch and pulled his shirt off and lifted one foot onto the couch, giving her better access to his ass.

"Is you?" She teasingly flicked her tongue across his asshole, and watched it pucker in response.

"Hell nah." He groaned and grabbed her by the back of the head and pressed her face back into his ass.

His eyes rolled into the back of his head. The fact that she ate his ass was another reason he'd never leave her alone.

Before Zyair met McKenzie, he never let a bitch anywhere near his ass. He wasn't with that gay shit, but he soon learned that when it came to McKenzie, she had no boundaries. If she wanted to do some-thing, she was going to do it, and whoever she was dealing with was going to like it. And after the first time she licked that spot and gave him a rim job, he was hooked.

Eating his ass is what got her the big ass condo with a stunning view, she was eating his ass in.

"Mmm, jack my dick, babe."

She did as he instructed and wrapped both of her hands around his length and stroked him while repeatedly swirling her tongue around his asshole. His sexy moans and groans made her pussy drip for him. She couldn't wait to feel him inside of her. One thing she absolutely loved was seeing Zyair's controlling ass, losing his shit as she sucked and fucked him the way only some type of sex demon could.

"Oh shit, I'm gonna blow." His hands reached around to cup around hers and jerk him faster.

McKenzie removed her tongue from his ass and wrapped her mouth around the head of his dick, anxiously waiting to taste him.

He groaned loudly and shot his load into her warm mouth. His toes curled, heart raced, and dick throbbed. She made him cum harder than any other bitch that he had ever fucked. His ass wasn't going anywhere.

After swallowing his load, she sexually licked her lips, smiling at the visual of Zyair in all of his black ass glory. Just scrumptious. He flashed her a boyish grin that reminded her of his youthful age. He was heavy in the streets, so it made him a lot older than what he was. That's what pressure from the streets did to a young nigga.

She fought the urge to grin back, and instead straddled his lap. His phone rang and they both looked at it to see his girl calling again. He flipped the phone so she couldn't see the screen and muted it.

"Don't worry about the phone. Come put that pussy in my face." He slapped her ass and watched her every movement while she climbed onto his face, mounting his tongue with a long moan.

Zyair wasted no time, stroking her large clit with gentle flicks. McKenzie had a bigger clit than any woman that he had ever been with. He used to think that it was a little weird. It was like licking on a small gumball, but he eventually embraced it and grew to love it.

Because her clit was so big, she was a lot more sensitive than any other woman he'd been with. Whenever he was licking on it, it made her go crazy on the dick after. It also helped that he genuinely enjoyed tasting her, especially since he didn't eat women out. Not even his fiancée. McKenzie though? That was some cake he'd never turn down. He devoured it every time.

His phone rang again, and a sneaky grin spread across her face. She leaned forward to grab his phone and answered it, putting it on speaker.

"Will you stop callin'?"

"You're one bold bitch. You just love being slutted out by my man, don't you?"

McKenzie laughed, and then moaned loudly when he pinched her clit between his thick, dark lips. "'The fuckin' boldest. I ain't the one being slutted out, baby. Why the fuck you think this nigga can't stay away from me?"

Zyair moaned against her flesh, his dick hardening at her talking

.

her shit. She was that bitch and couldn't nobody tell her shit. He loved it.

"Just because you're willing to let him treat you like some whore on the street doesn't mean anything, baby girl. At the end of the day, I'm the one that he put a ring on. This little thing y'all have going on won't last long. As soon as we're married, you'll be history, babe."

McKenzie laughed. She's delusional.

She hissed and ground her fat clit roughly against his wet tongue. She purposely moaned into the phone's mic.

"Girl, bye! You got that ring, because I didn't want it, bitch. Stop fucking playing with me. He's only your man because I let you have him, hoe!"

The more shit she talked, the harder he got, and the faster he ate her pussy. There was something so fucking sexy about his women fighting over him. He knew who his dick was rooting for, though.

"Yeah, you keep telling yourself that, sweetie. Will you put my man on the phone now?"

McKenzie moaned before responding. "Can't. He's eating and has his mouth full."

Zyair met her bronze eyes. She saw nothing but pure and unadulterated lust staring back at her. She grinned down at him.

He got off on her talking shit to his girl just as much as she did. She always knew just what he liked and how to help him take his orgasms to the next level.

"I'm gonna whoop your ass when I see you."

"I'm waiting hoe. You know where I be at." And with that, McKenzie hung up the phone and brushed one of her hands down the fade of his head.

Zyair gave her clit a few firm strokes with the tip of his tongue, and she imploded on his face.

"Why you so mean to my girl, Ken?" He asked when he unattached his lips from her pussy and licked and sucked the inside of her thighs.

"Why you let me be mean to your girl, Zy?" It was a legitimate question.

"Don't try to turn your fucked up-ness around on me."

"Ain't nobody doing shit. Every time you come around here

wanting me to fuck and suck on you, your bitch wants to come starting shit with me. So, you damn right I'm mean to that bitch. The fuck you think I am, Zy?"

Her toffee skin flushed red, a sign that she was getting upset. He got up from his seated position and pushed her onto her back and settled himself between her legs, lining his thick dick up at her entrance.

"You right. Imma check her when I get home." He rubbed the head of his dick teasingly back and forth across that juicy clit of hers.

"You better. I'd hate to have to cut you off." She threatened through a moan, her pussy leaking in anticipation for him to fill her.

"You gone cut me off?" He slowly sank into her. She was so tight, wet, and warm that he had to throw his head back and really enjoy the feel of what he was convinced to be the best pussy in the world. That tight muthafucka made him feel like he was the luckiest nigga in the world to be blessed with such a wonderful experience.

"I will if I have to." She moaned and used her thumb to thrum her clit.

He pushed her hand away and replaced it with his own and caught on to a rhythm and slowly long stroked her. He wanted her to feel every inch of his big dick and remember why she couldn't stop fucking him just as much as he wouldn't stop fucking her.

"Yeah? You don't want me to put this dick in your stomach no more?"

She said nothing, so he pulled completely out of her and then slammed back into her roughly. "Huh?"

"No," she said through a moan.

Zyair rolled his eyes and slapped her inner thigh. "You fulla shit, but okay."

He pulled out of her and stood to his feet. Smirking down at her and picking her up, he threw her over his shoulder and walked out to the balcony. The sun was starting to set, and the heat of the day was finally starting to cool down.

McKenzie giggled as she slumped over his shoulder. She didn't know why, but his ass loved tossing her around and she let him.

They were both butt ass naked as he rested her on her feet to look out at the amazing view of the city, at that time. She had neighbors that only needed to look out of their windows to see them, but they didn't give a fuck. They've fucked for audiences before.

Kenzie took a deep breath amazed at the view every time she was out there. She was grateful for it. Her hands gripped the iron railing, and her lips parted when she felt the heat of his body envelope her. One of his hands grabbed her hip, making her arch her back, and his other hand gripped his dick, as he fed it into her pussy.

Her body melted into him as soon as he entered her. He rested his face into the crook of her neck, holding her closely. The sounds of his moans in her ear making her wetter with every long, slow stroke.

"You like the view, baby?" He was curious.

He had been doing some house shopping with Kristina when he saw it. His fiancée didn't want any kids, so she wanted to move into a condo.

When they viewed it together, Kristina had fallen head over heels for the property. It was lavish, in a great area with a great view. Truly fit for a queen. Too bad she wasn't the queen he felt was worthy enough of it.

As soon as he stepped inside and saw the large open concept, updated appliances, and the balcony, he knew that he was going to cop it for McKenzie. He knew that she was going to love it, and she did. She sucked his dick and ate his ass extra nastily the night he picked her up and surprised her with it.

"I love it, Zyair. Thank you." She turned her head so that she could kiss him.

He thrusted into her harder, making her moan every time he hit bottom.

"The world is yours, baby." And she believed him.

She knew that if she asked him for anything, he wouldn't hesitate to give it to her. If she called, he came running. When it came down to it, Zyair was the most consistent and reliable person in her life.

"A nigga just wishes that he was able to wake up in this bitch with you every morning and slide in this pussy." His hand drifted between her legs, thrumming her clit again.

McKenzie clutched the railing tighter and moaned. "You 'bout to marry a whole different woman, Zy."

He pumped into her harder, applying pressure to both her g-spot and her mental. "Whose fault is that?"

"Not mine!" She tried to pull away from him, but instead he pushed her into the railing and forcefully bent her over it. Her eyes widened and her heart raced in her chest as she looked at the large, jagged edges of rocks fifteen feet below.

Zyair grabbed the railing, trapping her so that he could pound hard and fast into her. "Say the word, Kenz. Say it and I swear to God, I'll throw that bitch out like a dirty dish rag."

Her eyes rolled into the back of her head. He was hitting just the right spot that had her squirting all over his dick with each stroke. She didn't answer him just focused on how good he was making her feel.

"Look at this pussy wetting me up. You don't wanna wake up and go to sleep like this, Kenz? You don't want this?" He grabbed her around the throat and pulled her up so that her back was touching his chest.

She looked out at the view, and watched the sun set and all the city lights turn on in the distance as it began to darken. It was literally the most beautiful, erotic, and dare she say romantic thing she had experienced in her life. Tears welled in her eyes as she felt an orgasm swirling around in her gut, making her body tremble hard against him.

He had managed to get into her head, and she was fighting hard to not go there with him. She hated when he brought up them becoming more than what they were. She couldn't understand why he just couldn't keep things as they were.

"You don't want us, McKenzie?" His voice broke in the middle of his sentence.

"I'm cumming." Her words came out in a rush and through a moan as she let go.

Her orgasm prompted his and he released deep inside of her with a loud groan. The two took a few moments to catch their breaths.

"Why you don't wanna be with me, McKenzie? Why am I never good enough for you?" He pulled out of her and took a few steps back.

McKenzie remained in the same position against the balcony railing. She stared blankly out at the view in front of her, tears freely streaming down her face. She remained quiet. After a minute or two of silence, Zyair shook his head and turned to go back inside and put his clothes on. He knew that she wasn't going to answer him. She never did when he brought it up. And every time he did, his heart broke a little bit more each time.

He took his time showering and dressing. He was putting his Rolex back on his wrist when he emerged from her bedroom. McKenzie was on the couch nursing a drink, the sounds of H.E.R. playing softly from the speakers built into the ceiling throughout the place. She was in a satin robe with her toffee legs tucked beneath her. He wanted nothing more than to just stay and be with her. They didn't even have to fuck all night like they normally did. He just wanted to be held by her, while they went back and forth roasting each other.

But he needed to go. His feelings were hurt, and he didn't want her to know it. Shit, he brought it on himself. He knew that she wouldn't give him a real answer as to why she didn't want to be exclusively his. It never stopped him from asking in hopes that he had somehow proved that he was worthy of her heart.

He made his way over to the couch where he had left his phone. The two of them locked eyes when he neared her. She held his phone out for him to take.

"You're more than enough, Zyair. Always have been." Her voice was horse from crying.

"Then what's the problem?" He was genuinely confused.

She diverted her eyes, and he took a seat next to her on the couch and clasped his hands together.

"I'm the one who isn't good enough, Zy. Kristina though? She's good for you. Nice, gorgeous, intelligent, all of that. I don't have shit to offer you but ass."

In the two years he and McKenzie had been fucking around, he'd never heard her so sad and serious. He hated that she felt that way and was comparing herself to his girl when there was no need. It also didn't sit well with him that she kept downplaying herself. He had never known her to be the insecure type, but that's exactly how she sounded in that moment, and he felt guilty for it.

"That's not true," he protested.

She rolled her eyes and took a sip of her henny and coke. "It is, but okay. We don't even know each other like that and you talking about moving in here together."

His head jerked back. "Woah, we been fuckin' for two years, Kenz. How the hell do we not know each other? We ain't strangers, nigga."

"Exactly! We been fuckin'. That's it! We know nothing about each other outside of how we like to have sex."

His face was screwed up as he tried to process what she was saying. "That's bullshit."

She sighed and ran her fingers through her bundles. "What's my last name, Zyair?"

Silence.

She took another sip of her drink. "When's my birthday?"

"We celebrated your birthday together this year."

"Okay?" She raised an eyebrow at him and shifted so that she could look at him directly. "You should know when it is then, right?"

Damn. He had to think back and make a guess. "Uh, it's in March, right?" He scratched his head.

"No. You get my point, yet?"

He sighed and ran a hand down his face. "No. I never remember shit like that. That typa shit ain't important."

"That's why more will never be able to become of us, Zyair. That kind of shit is important to me. I don't wanna commit to you and then be disappointed that it's not all sugar and rainbows. There's a whole lot of shit that comes with fuckin' with a nigga like you. Being deemed yours in a city that you run will force me to be trapped in a bubble for many different reasons, none of which I'd care to experience."

"You know you've always been safe with me, McKenzie." That was a concern that he heard from women that he was involved with. It was a concern that Kristina constantly brought up to him when she tried to convince him to get out of the dope game and go legit.

His career of choice was in a dangerous industry. Niggas wanted his head everywhere he went and were willing to hurt anyone attached to him. The women he was with always wanted the benefits, but then got scared and ran when the risks got too risky. He thought that McKenzie was different and that she would be able to handle what came with his lifestyle. He was quickly becoming disappointed to know that everything that he had perceived her to be was the exact opposite.

"I'm not worried about street shit. I tote pistols too, nigga. I ain't never feared death. Six months ago, you proposed to me, and I said no. I didn't think you were ready for marriage. I still don't think you're ready. I don't even think that you are the marriage type at all. And you proved it to me when two months after turning you down, I look on fucking Instagram and see some preppy bitch with the ring you tried to give me on her finger, posted on your page."

She paused to calm herself down. Her voice was strained as she spoke, her emotions getting the best of her. He sat quietly, mentally kicking his own ass for the dumb shit that he had done.

"You like drama, Zyair. Cool, if that's what you want to do, fine. I get off on arguing and showing my ass in front of your bitches some-times, too. It's been fun. But I'm damn near thirty, this shit is getting old. My feelings are involved, and honestly, you giving that bitch my ring, hurt like hell. Being with you will mean that everybody knows that I'm yours. Therefore, making me off limits, cause the niggas in this city is mad pussy and never go against you. And at the same time, you can still, and more than likely will still be out in the streets doing you. I'm not that dumb of a bitch, Zyair. If we go there, I know for a fact that I will lose you the same damn way I got you. That's how karma works."

She finished off the rest of her drink.

He sighed and sat back against the couch, thinking. She had a few points. He wanted to tell her that she had everything wrong but figured that he should just keep it to himself until they were more emotionally under control.

"I'm just gonna go." He had a whole lot that he wanted to say, but the timing was off.

They needed some time apart, so he was going to give her that. She was nodding her head when he stood up. Her eyes were staring blankly out of the living room window, and she stayed in that position until she heard the front door close, and finally, she let the tears fall down her face.

Available Now
on all online retail book platforms!!

COMING SOON FROM

URBAN AINT DEAD

The Hottest Summer Ever 2
By **Elijah R. Freeman**

THE G-CODE
By **Elijah R. Freeman**

How To Publish A Book From Prison
By **Elijah R. Freeman**

Tales 4rm Da Dale 2
By **Elijah R. Freeman**

Ridin' For You, Too
By **Telia Teanna**

Hittaz 3
By **Lou Garden Price, Sr.**

The State's Witness 2
By **Kyiris Ashley**

The Swipe 2
By **Toōla**

A Setup For Revenge 2
By **Ashley Williams**

Good Girl Gone Rogue 2
By **Manny Black**

Charge It To The Game 2
By **Nai**

Despite The Odds 2
By **Juhnell Morgan**

Stuck In The Trenches 2
By **Huff Tha Great**

OTHER BOOKS BY

URBAN AINT DEAD

Tales 4rm Da Dale
By **Elijah R. Freeman**

The Hottest Summer Ever
By **Elijah R. Freeman**

Despite The Odds
By **Juhnell Morgan**

The Swipe
By **Toōla**

Hittaz 1 & 2
By **Lou Garden Price, Sr**

Good Girls Gone Rogue
By **Manny Black**

The State's Witness
By **Kyiris Ashley**

Ridin' For You
By **Telia Teanna**

A Setup For Revenge
By **Ashley Williams**

Charge It To The Game

By **Nai**

BOOKS BY

URBAN AINT DEAD's C.E.O

Elijah R. Freeman

Triggadale 1, 2 & 3

Tales 4rm Da Dale

The Hottest Summer Ever

Murda Was The Case 1 & 2

Follow

Elijah R. Freeman

On Social Media

FB: Elijah R. Freeman

IG: @the_future_of_urban_fiction

Made in the USA
Middletown, DE
29 April 2023